no time
to
garden
the
half-hour
gardener

Anne Swithinbank

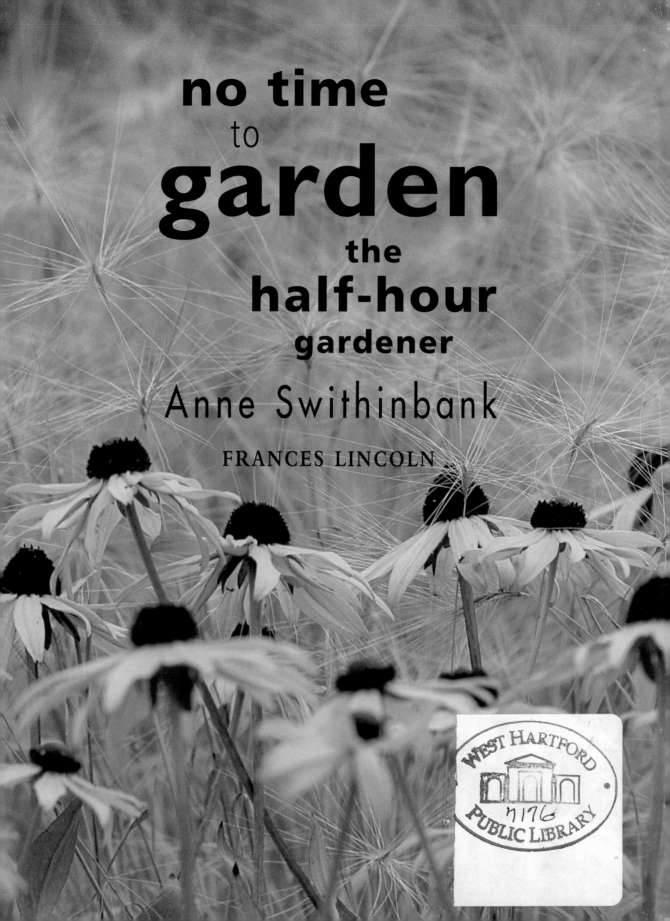

no time
to
garden
the
half-hour
gardener

Anne Swithinbank

FRANCES LINCOLN

For John, my husband, and all the family for their
willingness to act as sounding boards for ideas and
for general, unstinting support. And for my friends
who think they have no time to garden.

Frances Lincoln Limited
4 Torriano Mews
Torriano Avenue
London NW5 2RZ

No Time to Garden
Copyright © Frances Lincoln Limited 2002
Original text copyright © Anne Swithinbank
Photographs copyright © Mark Bolton except for
those on the following pages:
© John Glover 11, 16, 17, 115 & 119
Andrew Lawson 69 (Gothic House, Charlbury,
Oxford), 139 above right
Juliette Wade 13 (Joe and Jerry Eveley, London)
First Frances Lincoln edition 2002

British Library Cataloguing in Publication Data
A catalogue record for this book is available from
the British Library
ISBN 0 7112 1681 9
9 8 7 6 5 4 3 2 1

Printed and bound in Singapore

Q
635.9
SWITHIN-
BANK

PREVIOUS PAGES Simple, fashionable and low-
maintenance: the daisy heads of *Rudbeckia fulgida*
var. *sullivantii* 'Goldsturm' amid the swaying stems
of the grass *Hordeum jubatum*.

contents

introduction 6

planting projects 78

planting basics 20

seasonal maintenance 36

easy-care plants 122

the living garden 156

index 171   acknowledgments 176

introduction

SO MANY PEOPLE LONG TO IMMERSE THEMSELVES IN THEIR GARDENS, yet have convinced themselves that they have 'no time to garden'. We all hit busy patches in our lives when caring for small children, juggling a family with a career, running a business or other commitments can seem to take over, leaving precious little time for anything else. Yet gardening offers the time-pressed the most wonderful opportunities to switch off and slow down. My mission is to convince the aspiring gardener with 'no time' that it is still possible to enjoy taking care of your plot.

My 'no-time' philosophy has grown out of personal experience. Although I am a professional gardener, I now earn most of my living by writing and talking about gardening, and the days of physically gardening for eight hours are long gone. With two young children, a busy household to run and a job to do, I very rarely have the luxury of an uninterrupted full day, or even half a day to spend working in my own garden. Much of my gardening is crammed into half-hour snatches of time, stolen between one task and another. Nevertheless, I do manage to make improvements, and each one feels like a triumph. Even though I am short of time, I know every plant in my garden, as well as the garden's own idiosyncrasies of climate and soil. It is far from perfect, but I take great pleasure in the fact that I am myself in control of its destiny.

Given sufficient determination, anyone can release the odd half-hour. And anyone with a sufficiently relaxed attitude can become a successful half-hour gardener. In this book I hope to show you a new, gentler way of perceiving the garden, where imperfections are allowed, rules are less rigid and easier to follow, and gardening in half-hour stretches is a real possibility. By half an hour I mean not half an hour a week, or half an hour a day, but half an hour whenever you can. For example, pruning five rose bushes can seem a mammoth task, but you might be able to find half an hour to prune one. The next time you have half an hour you can prune the next. Proceed like this and you will be surprised how soon you have five pruned bushes. Another half-hour spent weeding, feeding and mulching, and you will be set up for a summer of beautiful blooms.

I hope also to show you how to maximize precious time by gardening efficiently. As a time-pressed gardener you need to be well organized and ready to eliminate all but the most necessary tasks. You need to relax and acknowledge that radical changes are not going to happen overnight. Above all, you need to believe that every little really does count. Gentle, persistent improvements are the mantra of the gardener short of time. As you gradually take control of your garden, the incentive to do more will grow, and half-hour gardening will become addictive.

Relaxing in a deck chair may seem an indulgence when jobs need doing.
But you can use the time constructively to observe the garden and so be
better prepared when you have the chance to work on it.

introduction

Getting to know your garden

Nothing troubles the gardener with no time to garden more than guilt. But there is no rule that says every garden should be permanently tidy. A state of dishevelment suits some gardens, so resist the urge to fill every spare moment with physical labour.

It is important to remember that most gardens are beautiful, whatever their state of repair. Enjoy your garden even if you have no time to work in it. Unless it is an empty plot, it will surely have something – the previous owner's planting, a beautiful tree – to enjoy. I can remember taking pleasure from my last garden in its original, ramshackle state. I permitted myself a year's grace, during which I enjoyed, for instance, the blossom of its elderly fruit trees, carpeted beneath with cow parsley and bluebells in spring. Birds of all kinds found a haven in overgrown mock oranges and flowering currants.

All of us spend time in the garden not gardening – perhaps we are entertaining visitors, maybe we feel there is not enough time to get stuck into a job, or perhaps we need to relax. Never think of sitting or wandering about as a waste of time; view these moments of leisure as valuable opportunities to inspect your garden and to learn about it. Even moving your chair to a fresh spot will reveal new pleasures – a close-up of a plant or a different viewpoint. It is amazing how much you can learn about your garden just by being in it, at different times of the day and year. This is when your imagination is likely to be fired and inspirations strike. Use these moments to note down problems in need of solving and the most urgent jobs. Then you can focus on the priorities when you do get the chance to up tools.

Getting to know your garden is important if you are to use any time you have in it wisely. Whether

Instant improvements are possible by rearranging props. A quick wander around the garden revealed this sunny, sheltered site begging for a seat and some added fragrance

and colour. Raking out leaves and twigs and smoothing the gravel took about ten minutes. Arranging the wooden bench and pots from other parts of the garden took no time at all.

you have just taken on a garden, or you have resolved to try again with an existing plot, do take some time to acquaint or reacquaint yourself with it before you begin work on it.

Notice where the sun shines throughout the year and at different times of the day, and which areas of the garden are shaded. Pinpoint sheltered nooks – and the cold places where frost lingers longest. See how the garden is affected by wind, tempered and channelled by hedges, buildings and walls. Take note of badly placed plants or those not flourishing. Studying your plot in this way will help you make good decisions in your gardening, saving both time and money. Even in small, seemingly predictable gardens, there may lurk surprises, both pleasant and unpleasant – hidden views, buried bulbs, which will affect future plans you make for the garden.

Adopting a suitable style

Everyone has their own personal style and one of the best things about gardening is the pleasure of expressing and developing this. Analyse your style by reading books and magazines and visiting other gardens. This will make you decisive and save a lot of trial and error. I prefer a classic, informal garden with leanings towards wildness, planted and gardened to attract wildlife. This is convenient, because within reason I can tolerate and even justify some rough edges. Formal styles tend to be high-maintenance, but you can create the look by repetition, creative clipping and paired containers. A tropical scene can be achieved with large-leaved but hardy foliage plants, possibly with the addition of a few tender, high-maintenance cannas or bananas. Even colourful, old-fashioned bedding can be grown in carefully managed sweeps positioned between low-maintenance shrubs and perennials. Have

Now reaching its peak, this border of large herbaceous plants including masses of pink astilbe has been given structure throughout the growing season by the rustic 'wigwam' or cone, with a Chilean glory flower (*Eccremocarpus scaber*) twining about it. Erecting and planting up a woven willow or hazel support like this is quick to achieve (see page 106); even making your own wigwam out of hazel sticks would be possible over a few half-hours.

vegetables, but just slot a few in here and there. Keep hedges, but choose low-maintenance types (such as yew and beech) which can be cut once a year with a power trimmer.

Although you should be guided by your personal taste, remember that a successful garden is usually one that sits comfortably in its immediate environment, whether that consists of buildings, streets or countryside. There is no law to stop anyone from making the garden of their dreams, but an extravagantly unusual approach can stick out like a sore thumb among a row of otherwise similar gardens. In the countryside, or among other gardens in a town or city, you have a borrowed landscape and can harness surrounding views and vistas in your garden design. Owners of small, hemmed-in courtyards, however, can enjoy the freedom of self-controlled isolation. They can create anything they like and get away with it.

Planning

Once you have decided on an overall style for the garden, it is worth making some plans and lists, however basic.

If a complete redesign seems unavoidable, you will need some help, because implementing major changes is time-consuming and beyond the remit of this book. But even the gardener with no time should be able to care for and fine-tune the finished product. When I developed my old garden, I was able to redesign it completely, creating new lawns and borders, because my husband worked with me. Had this not been possible we could have gradually removed the oldest of the trees and shrubs and renovated others. In fact I could have enjoyed the original, overgrown version almost as much by leaving it alone and making much smaller changes. A lot of the wildness could have been retained and even added to, by planting hawthorns, elderflowers and buddlejas to attract birds and butterflies, with grassy areas mown to create glades.

Maintenance should be taken into account when choosing plants (see page 13), and when incorporating features such as lawns (see page 12) or hedges. Consider whether you might have help with routine maintenance tasks such as mowing and hedge-trimming that are easy to delegate. Be constantly aware of the limitations imposed by time and plan to get rid of awkward features like old, weed-infested rock gardens and silly strips of lawn. Some expanses of border might be better grassed or paved over to reduce maintenance. Evaluate what is important to you: containers, for instance, once planted, will need watering, but in my view it is worth spending time on preparing a few pots for each season as they help brighten up the garden and create an instant effect.

In designing your garden, there are a few golden rules. A jumble of plants and artefacts stuck here and there will not only look confusing, but will be a nightmare to maintain. Try to plant in drifts of several of one sort of plant and use focal points such as pots and water features sparingly and in ways that blend with each other. Sticking with a basic style, rather than mixing touches of Mediterranean, Oriental and wildflower meadow all in the same small area, will be less time-consuming as well as more effective. The age-old formula of having a more formal garden round the house, which becomes ever softer and wilder further away from the house, works well in tiny plots as well as large ones.

This is my previous garden, which, apart from the old apple tree, looked nothing like this when we took it on. Creating a new garden from a neglected plot was time-consuming, but once the lawn had settled (it was seeded) and the ground had been covered by plants, its maintenance was relatively straightforward. Plantings could be developed in half-hour projects, such as planting tulip bulbs during autumn or adding ferns under the apple tree.

Lawns and the time-pressed gardener

Whether lawns are high or low maintenance is the basis of many gardening arguments. I love lawns in gardens, because of their cool, soft green surface, which set off the rest of the garden, enhancing both soil and plants. No other surfacing material feels as good to bare feet. But for some owners, lawns can be the stuff of nightmares because of sprouting weeds, bare patches or moss – though why these should be regarded as such a source of horror, I am not sure.

The perfect lawn, about which whole books have been written, is attainable, but not by the time-pressed gardener. In any case, for a lawn to be an asset, it does not need to be perfect, just healthy

Learning to live with a weedy lawn has its compensations — as when the grass erupts into sprinklings of pretty white daisies. So long as the turf is strong enough to grow despite them, daisies can be viewed as an asset, not a problem. Here, with plantings of white-flowered alliums near by, these daisies create a semi-wild vision of a white garden.

and strong. Weeds and moss will creep into most lawns, but as long as the surface remains more or less green and flat, you need not consider these a problem. Learn to love the variety of your lawn, and the rich character of its grasses and wildflowers could turn out to be a delight. The nicest are speedwell (small light blue flowers), selfheal (purple-blue flowers) and daisies. Clover offers the prospect of a lucky four-leaved find, is a great favourite with grazing pet rabbits and by returning nitrogen to the soil fertilizes the lawn, while moss gives lawns a lovely spongy texture. I enjoy the rich tapestry of plants which make up my turf, especially as in my garden I am lucky to have large grassy areas that receive plenty of light in an area of high rainfall on a rich soil.

Deciding not to use weedkillers can be liberating. You save time by not having to buy, store and apply them. There are no worries about when to allow children and pets back on to the lawn or the problem of adding weedkillers to the compost heap along with the clippings.

For the gardener with limited time, a robust lawn is a useful blanket to cover large tracts of garden which would otherwise require a hard surface or need to be developed with plants and other features (both time-consuming and expensive). Delegate mowing and edging to others if possible; then you will only have to deal with minor problems (see pages 50–51).

Real problem lawns occur in places where there is shade and bad drainage and poor soil, where weeds and moss tend to flourish at the expense of the grasses. If you have such a lawn, you would be well advised to give up on it. One of the easiest replacements is a soil bed, planted up, then mulched with a thick layer of shingle (see page 66). If conditions are still too harsh for plants, you could place containers of good soil on the shingle.

Choosing plants

Choosing plants from the tens of thousands available can be a time-consuming task. To help you, I have provided a selection (see pages 122–55) which I consider to be useful and easy-going for busy gardeners, with basic information about them. The symbol ♕ denotes those that have been given the Royal Horticultural Society's Award of Garden Merit. The information on each plant includes the conditions it needs to thrive, as choosing the right plant for the right place is vital for success. My main criterion for selecting plants was that they should be unfussy, needing no particular pampering, feeding, special soils or staking. All should settle quickly and, as far as possible, keep going from year to year. A few that require more maintenance, such as wisteria, are included because they are excellent value in the garden. As most gardeners will have limited opportunities for planting larger trees or shrubs, I have focused on smaller ones and chosen those which give a long season of interest.

Everything we need to know about planting is in the natural landscape. In woods, for instance, there is an obvious canopy or top layer provided by the largest, or forest, trees such as beech, oak, ash and chestnut. Next down is an understorey of smaller trees and large shrubs, which might include deciduous hazel and evergreen holly. The forest floor can hold a variety of plants, many of them bulbs, such as bluebells. A heath might be home to pines and birches with underplantings of heather and interesting grasses. Old-fashioned wildflower meadows and grasslands provide a delightful display of grasses mixed with annuals and perennials. Seaside plantings of teasel, viper's bugloss and horned poppy give an insight as to how plants can look wonderful growing out of shingle. Use natural plantings such as these to inspire you with ideas and help you visualize plants in your garden.

The owners of this city courtyard garden decided to grow exotic plants which, although mainly in containers, give year-round value and need a lot less care than the flowers they replaced. The mainly evergreen plants need little maintenance and enjoy the insulating effect of surrounding buildings; only the banana plants and tree ferns need protection from frost. Colour is introduced in summer with paired pots of bright red pelargoniums where steps lead to the garden.

Choose trees and larger shrubs first, combining deciduous types that lose their leaves in autumn with evergreens, for a variety of twiggy outlines and bold foliage. Aim to select a combination capable of bringing colour to the garden all year. Apples and pears are among my favourites for the blossom and fruit they offer, as well as attracting a lot of

introduction

13

wildlife. Or you might opt for trees with attractive bark, such as the moosewood and birches. Amelanchiers and rowans pay triple rent for they provide blossom, fruit and autumn colour. Always choose with a particular atmosphere or style in mind. For instance, where there is a formal look and bright aspect to a garden, with a lot of aromatics like rosemary and lavender, think grand Italian gardens and add a few pencil-thin cypresses or an upright, slender Irish yew.

When planting trees and shrubs, make sure that they will have enough space around them to grow to maturity. We may only occupy gardens for relatively short spaces of time, but it is nice to think that we leave behind a legacy of plantings that should long outlive our tenancies. Spaces between the major plants can be filled with smaller shrubs, herbaceous perennials, biennials and annuals. These will be shorter lived and their pattern may change many times as the larger plants mature. Smaller shrubs like aromatic caryopteris are ideal for filling gaps for six or seven years while larger shrubs are growing, but they can be grubbed out with no compunction when they become straggly and are squeezed for space.

If trees and shrubs provide the bones of a garden, then perennials – plants whose stems do not become woody and are not permanent – flesh them out. Most die back for the winter, but grow again from their crowns of dormant buds in spring. Some herbaceous perennials are evergreen, such as the marvellous, silvery-leaved *Helleborus argutifolius*, but the leaves eventually die off in spring to

Areas of garden left natural for reasons of time-economy can be made to look more organized and cared for by plantings of semi-wild plants like these foxgloves. Biennials, they can either be raised in a seedbed and transplanted, or bought and planted out in early autumn.

be replaced by a new set. Perennials are at their most spectacular in bold drifts of one sort, flowing between other plants. This is easily achieved, even on a tight budget, because one original plant will grow and spread in such a way that it can easily be pulled apart into several new pieces (see page 34). Grasses and ferns are great gap fillers too.

Although perennials are a safe bet for the time-pressed gardener, as they do not need frequent replacement, be sure not to overlook the shorter-lived biennials, tender perennials and annuals, which have great fun value. These plants add variety to the garden because, by their ephemeral nature, they tempt us to experiment and ring the changes every year. Biennials such as honesty, foxgloves, sweet rocket, some verbascums, clary sage and wallflowers are grown from seed sown during the spring of one year, spend the rest of the year building up into a big, healthy rosette of

growth, then during the spring or early summer of their second season, they explode into flower, before setting seed and dying. Buying these ready grown in early autumn is the quickest and easiest way of enjoying them, but do try sowing one or two kinds from seed sown into a small seedbed (see page 24).

Tender perennials have the capacity to live a long life, but only under the tender ministrations of the time-rich hobby gardener with a greenhouse. Forget this, but buy a few in late spring – perhaps some marguerites, tender lavenders and fragrant heliotropes – to fill gaps for the summer.

Annuals – plants that grow from seed during spring, bloom in summer, produce and shed seed, then die – are divided into two sorts. The raising of half-hardy annuals is, again, best left to professionals and gardeners with plenty of time. But buy them as bedding plants in late spring, planting them out

when all danger of frost has past. Most are highly bred to guarantee a good performance whether they are deadheaded or not, but it is worth spending time cutting off the fading flowerheads if you can, because if you do, the plant seems to realize that it has not yet shed any seed and redoubles its efforts to make more flowers. Hardy annuals are generally more wild-looking and can be sown straight into the soil during spring (see page 25). Poppies, love-in-a-mist, clarkia and cornflowers will often seed themselves around successfully, finding their own gaps to grow in year after year.

Even when a section of border is colonized by plants, it can be further improved by adding more layers. For instance, a group of dogwoods, grown for their winter stems, can be complemented by planting through them perennials such as campanulas and rudbeckias, whose stems will be supported by the dogwoods and will in turn brighten them up for summer. A group of winter heathers can be improved in summer by adding *Clematis* x *durandii* whose stems (they do not cling) can be pegged between the plants and will then dazzle with large blue flowers. Bulbs can be added to grow through all kinds of plants, such as tulips to flower in spring or alliums for early summer.

There are plenty of plants to furnish the ground below and between shrubs. The likes of bergenia, named elephant's ears on account of their large evergreen leaves, the small evergreen shrub *Euonymus fortunei* 'Emerald 'n' Gold' and lady's mantle (*Alchemilla mollis*) will give impenetrable, reliable weed-suppressing ground cover. Grasses, ferns and delectable subjects like maroon-flowered *Knautia macedonica*, pulmonarias and hardy geraniums are also good at holding their own.

Climbing plants are obvious candidates for walls, fences, pergolas and arches, whatever their orientation, but can also be added to existing

planting. Clematis, the blue and white Chilean potato vines (*Solanum crispum* and *S. laxum* (syn. *S. jasminioides)* respectively), honeysuckles, sweet peas and even climbing and rambling roses can make great companions as long as they are not allowed to swamp. Always plant a companion climber in its own space to the side of the host plant and not so that the roots of the two are competing. You can then guide growth in the right direction. Choose climbers with flower colours to complement the shrubs behind them, or to extend the flowering season.

Though a thorough read of the plant directory will set you on the right road for choosing plants, your final selection will usually depend on what is available at the garden centre. To find a wider range of plants, take advantage of mail order, or arrange a day out to a major garden show where specialist nurseries sell plants. Always opt for plants which are tough and amenable and keep well away from

Easy self-seeders: a gift of variegated honesty seed gave rise to this magnificent show, flourishing in semi-shade under an apple tree and in full sun. Seed from these plants and their offspring will continue to give pleasure for years to come.

trickier subjects, especially if you are not sure if you have the right conditions for them. Choose plants for quality and health. Look for plenty of vigorous shoots, avoiding anything wobbly, damaged or scruffy-looking and pot-bound plants which could have been hanging around for a while.

The half-hour principle

So how to go about creating your own personal haven? This is where you employ the half-hour principle. The problem with making your debut as a half-hour gardener is that no one tells the plants (and weeds) that this is the plan. Life would be easy if one's starting point were a well-maintained garden, but in reality there are usually hundreds of jobs lined up at once. I would classify these into two types. The most satisfying are neat, self-contained half-hour jobs with a beginning and an end. Recently I spent half an hour digging, cutting and pulling a bramble out of a beautiful flowering viburnum. On another occasion, using a bladed gadget to dig weeds and grasses out of a section of path gave quick results. Planting a packet of tulip bulbs or one shrub to fill a gap would also fit into this category.

More challenging are larger tasks and projects taking several half-hours to complete. When confronted with a large, untidy border, the temptation might be to prune all the shrubs first, then complete the weeding, then move on to lifting and dividing perennials and finally to adding new plants. But trying to achieve all this on a limited time budget is going to be soul-destroying and it may be months before you have anything to show for your efforts. I would take an overview of the whole border, then split it into sections and complete one at a time. Don't worry about how wild the others are becoming in the meantime, and don't move on until you are sure the completed sections can be well maintained.

Where funds allow, it might be tempting to call in contractors to clear and tidy, but my advice is to get stuck in. This way, you can have everything done how you want, learn loads in the process and start building that special, rewarding relationship between gardener and garden.

Getting started

If you have not done much gardening for some time, your first effort might feel like persuading a rusty old wheel to turn, and you might find that you do not get as much done as you had hoped. But do not be discouraged. Once you become more experienced, you will achieve more in each half-hour.

The border shown here was nothing like this when it was first planted – for instance, the *Lychnis coronaria* (foreground) and *Salvia forsskaolii* (behind) started as one demure plant each, positioned neatly in the middle. Once it had sorted itself out it looked a lot better. The secrets of encouraging borders to care for themselves include thoughtful initial planting, avoiding unnecessary soil disturbance (which disrupts the growth of seedlings), regularly pullling up weeds before they seed, and occasionally moving, adding or subtracting a plant. That was all I had time for here. Over a two- to three-year period complete anarchy ensued, but with lovely results.

The first step is to decide that a particular job needs doing. Let us take as an example a simple project: to fill an empty corner by planting a good-sized shrub. The next step is to gather information. Take a notebook and begin by observing the corner more closely, jotting down a few points. When does sunlight shine there? Would it be described as bright and sunny, in semi-shade or full shade? What is the soil like? What shrub would be suitable? What should be its maximum size? Should it be evergreen or deciduous? Is the site so weedy that you will have to spend half an hour clearing before you can plant?

Even the busiest people have periods of inactivity or waste time. While commuting or having a lunch break, or instead of flaking out after work or chilling out to daytime TV while the baby sleeps, do some research. Read EASY-CARE PLANTS (pages 122–55) for inspiration; look at PLANTING BASICS for how to plant a shrub (page 28).

After jotting down some plant ideas, think tools and equipment. Preparation is bound to include some initial weeding, so a fork and bucket would be useful (and also gloves). A boundary hedge might need clipping, in which case, shears. Then a spade to dig the hole with. Make a list of any new tools you need. You will need to add soil conditioner, so make a note to buy a bagful of this. The soil may be poor, so note down tree and shrub fertilizer. You might also need a few ground-cover plants to make sure weeds do not colonize around the base. At the next opportunity, spend half an hour in your shed rummaging around for tools on the list. If you own a wheelbarrow, load the tools into it.

The final part of your preparation is shopping. Save time by combining gardening with your usual shopping rounds and be focused. Garden centres are full of diversions, but do not be diverted: go straight to the sections you need. For this job, I might select a silvery-leaved evergreen *Elaeagnus* x *ebbingei* as the main shrub, with three white winter-flowering heathers as ground-cover plants to go beneath and a packet of *Scilla siberica* bulbs to come up between them. If the plants you want

Not every job can be done in half an hour. This section of border was so rough and weedy with deep-rooted grass, ground elder and ivy that it took a week of half-hours, one a day, to get to this point. After each session, I simply cleaned my tools, popped them in the barrow and stored them in the shed for next time. Gradually I had the satisfaction of seeing the area clear and knowing that, as I had done the job properly, it would be a long time before I had to weed again.

are not there, settle for something similar, as shopping around is a time-consuming luxury. Seek advice if needed. At home, leave the plants outside, ensuring they do not dry out, until you are ready to plant them. With all your preparations completed, including a preliminary weeding if necessary, you are ready to wheel out your barrow and get planting (see pages 26 and 28).

Once you become practised in thinking in this way, you will have less need for careful preparation. By learning to think ahead, even when you are not actually gardening, you will be able to make the

introduction

most of any short time you actually spend in the garden. As you and your garden become more organized, you will be able to achieve more in a short space of time.

Using this book

The three 'doing' chapters in this book show you how to tackle a number of garden jobs and projects within roughly half an hour.

PLANTING BASICS describes general methods of introducing new plants into the garden – such as planting up containers – which you can use at any time with the plants of your choice.

SEASONAL MAINTENANCE explains the basic maintenance that might need tackling, in the form of half-hour tasks. These tasks are somewhat open-ended: they indicate how much can be achieved in half an hour, but it would be silly to pretend that every job will only take this long. So for a large job, such as pruning a huge wisteria, think in terms of taking several half-hours to complete the task, even if it stretches over a three-week period.

Some of the methods and suggestions might raise a few eyebrows in the correct school of gardening. The pruning of shrubs, for instance, is pared right down to a basic method which can be used on virtually any kind of shrub, at any time of the year. This saves you from spending hours you cannot spare with your nose in an encyclopaedia trying to identify what plant you have and what wood it flowers on.

The tasks include maintenance for plants you might already have in your garden, as I am not expecting anyone to uproot and dispose of a beautiful, huge wisteria, for instance, because pruning is too time-consuming. Although most jobs will mean working on just a small area, some, such as supporting perennials, are ones to be done around the whole garden at one time.

PLANTING PROJECTS describes small, self-contained improvements in which features or plants, or both, are added to the garden. Some are pure additions, like structures to add height. Others are plantings to augment features like trees and ponds which might already be in the garden. It should be possible to complete these within half an hour. You can allow them to stray into several sessions, but bear in mind that they work best if finished quickly.

Tips for busy gardeners

• Complete one task or project at a time and avoid starting another until you have finished.

• If you do not finish a task in half an hour, simply pack up and return again for another short session until that job is finished.

• Never try to dig a planting hole in compacted, unconditioned soil. This will feel like the hard work it is, the hole is unlikely to be deep enough and the plant will possibly not take. Taking time to dig or fork over the area beforehand, and incorporate soil conditioner and a handful of slow-release fertilizer (see page 22), will save time in the long run.

• When pruning shrubs, save any long twiggy pieces to use as plant supports. Tie together firmly into bundles and store in a dry place until needed.

• Where a lot of soil is open and you are unable to deal with it all at once, cover it with black polythene to exclude light and prevent weed growth.

• Learn to become fascinated rather than horrified by pests and diseases. They are not always the disaster they first appear to be. Most plants can survive blemishes on their leaves without dying. If you do use pesticides, buy them in ready-to-use form to save the time and effort of measuring, mixing and cleaning the sprayer afterwards.

• The quickest method of dealing with persistent problems is to get rid of the susceptible plant and replace it with something more robust.

planting basics

preparing the soil 22

sowing seeds 24

planting bulbs 26

planting into borders 28

planting a tree 30

planting up a container 32

easy propagation 34

0

10

15

20

25

30

preparing the soil

BY EXPECTING PLANTS FROM ACROSS the globe to take root and flourish in our gardens, we are attempting extraordinary things. Despite this, most soils will support a wide range of plants if they are properly conditioned. Adding quantities of well-decomposed, bulky, fibrous organic matter opens up the soil, makes it easier to cultivate, and helps it to retain moisture without becoming waterlogged. The extremes are sandy soils, through which water, nutrients and humus will slip rapidly, and heavy clay, which binds into solid lumps whether wet or dry. Even these can be improved by regular additions of soil conditioners, mulches (see page 66) and, for heavy clay, sharp grit. If for some reason a garden lacks a decent layer of topsoil (the workable, upper layers of a soil), it can be bought in by the sackful or delivered loose (usually 10 tons at a time). See also THE SOIL AND ITS CONTENT, page 160.

After a bed has been dug and planted, an annual mulch will be all it needs. Spread this a good 8cm/3in thick over the soil surface between the plants. There is no need to fork it in.

Why dig?

Few gardeners have time for laborious digging, and where soil is workable and reasonably free of perennial weeds, it can be avoided. Whether or not to dig is easily determined by how easily planting holes can be made. If fork and spade slide in comfortably, do not bother with digging. But if the soil is so compacted that any kind of penetration requires a crowbar, then dig. With single digging (described opposite), you break up and turn over the soil to the depth of a spade (called a 'spit'), and also break up the underlying soil with a fork. In the process you can pull out perennial weeds, bury annual weeds and grasses and add soil conditioner. Good soil and that which has been previously dug should not require digging again for many years if you avoid trampling it. Improve it on a regular basis by spreading a soil conditioner 8–10cm/3–4in thick and forking it into the top layers prior to planting.

Soil conditioners

The following conditioners give the best results:

Garden compost Recycling waste from the garden and kitchen eliminates the effort required to bag it up and dispose of it, and provides free, good-quality soil conditioner on site (see pages 162–3).

Leaf mould Made separately from garden compost, this is great for adding to lightly shaded or woodland-style beds. It adds fertility, creates a more open structure and holds moisture. It often has a slight acidifying effect, useful for acid-loving plants like rhododendrons and camellias.

Well-rotted manure Horse manure is available in most areas, though tracking it down, bagging it up and transporting it home can be time-consuming and potentially car-wrecking; the more expensive alternative is to have it delivered. All manure must be well rotted (when it becomes dark, crumbly and definitely not smelly) and free of pernicious weeds such as bindweed and ground elder.

Composted bark This and other proprietary conditioners are readily available from garden centres, but can be expensive to buy ready bagged (see also MULCHING, pages 66–7).

Spent mushroom compost A useful, fibrous by-product of the mushroom-growing. However, it is usually alkaline and not suitable for applying around acid-loving plants.

Digging a border

The soil in this section of border is compacted and needs a thorough digging over. In half an hour, you might tackle an area 2sq.m/40sq.ft, or half that if the going is heavy or if the bed is especially weedy. If you have a larger area to dig, divide the bed into rectangular strips about 1.8m/6ft wide, which you can work on as and when you have a spare half-hour.

When digging, use the soil from the the next strip of earth to cover the soil conditioner in the previous trench.

What you need
- wheelbarrow, spade, fork
- soil conditioner

How to do it
1 At one end of the bed dig out a trench across its width, to one spade depth and width. Put removed soil from this first trench in the wheelbarrow as you go and save until the end.
2 Now fork the base of the trench thoroughly to break up any hard lumps of soil and remove pieces of rubble or root, especially from perennial weeds.
3 Fork some soil conditioner into the base and up the sides of the trench to a depth of about 15cm/6in.
4 Cover this trench by turning the next spade width of soil over into it, creating a second trench. Repeat the forking, and add soil conditioner.
5 Carry on digging trenches in this way until gradually the whole area has been dug over.
6 Use the soil in the barrow to fill the final trench.

Aftercare
- Inevitably a freshly dug area will be higher after digging and it is wise to leave it for a few weeks before planting to allow settling to take place.
- Leaving the bed for a few weeks also allows weed seeds brought to the surface time to germinate. They can then be hoed off before planting.
- If you are in a hurry to plant, settle the soil quickly by treading it, then 'tickle' the surface with a fork or rake.

TIP When digging over a weedy bed or converting an area of lawn to bed, use the spade to slice off a 5cm/2in layer of soil containing weed roots or turf and place upside down in the bottom of the first trench. Bury under the next spitfuls of soil as you go; the grass and roots act as a soil conditioner, strengthening the soil's texture.

planting basics

23

RAISING PLANTS FROM SEED IS AN EASY, SATISFYING AND CHEAP way to stock a garden. The time-pressed gardener can adopt the most straightforward method: sowing seeds of hardy plants straight into the soil. This is a good way to start off vegetables, annuals (such as nasturtiums, love-in-a-mist, sunflowers), biennials (foxgloves, honesty, sweet rocket) and herbaceous perennials (lupins, bergamot, agastache). Plants sown straight into the soil and not moved are able to put down deep roots, making them stronger and more drought-tolerant – an advantage they will always have over their pot-raised siblings.

Sowing French beans

You don't need a vegetable patch to raise crops. In this border, there is a spare bare patch of soil to the front which French beans will fill, giving not only flowers but handfuls of tasty beans. If the soil is dry, water the whole area well the night before and leave to soak in.

What you need
• fork, rake, short length of cane
• bean seeds (the variety 'Delinel' is reliable; or use a mixture)
• pea sticks, label

How to do it
1 Gently tickle the soil with a fork, removing any weeds. Rake to and fro over the patch to create a (mostly) stone-free tilth.
2 With the cane, mark out straight, shallow drills 2.5cm/1in deep and 15cm/6in apart (**A**).
3 Place bean seeds in the drills 5cm/2in apart (**B**).
4 Use your hands to gently cover the seeds with soil (**C**) to a depth of little more than their own size. Pat the surface to firm.

5 Push pea sticks in around the outside of the area at angles, so they lean over the sown area (**D**). These stop cats digging or rolling in the seedbed. Place the label.

Aftercare
• Beans sown this way do not need thinning, so let all the seedlings mature.
• Take steps to control slugs and snails, particularly just after germination and before the plants toughen up (see page 168).
• When the beans are ready, pick regularly even if they are not needed to encourage more to set. Wrapped in polythene in the fridge they keep for several days.
• Water during dry spells, especially when beans are setting.

TIP A mix of varieties such as 'Purple Queen' and yellow wax 'Mont d'Or' yields different-coloured flowers as well as beans.

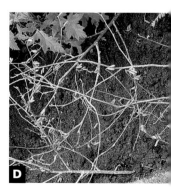

Sowing annual flower seeds

There are two methods of sowing. Both require the same careful soil preparation: forking over the soil, removing weeds, bashing out lumps and drawing a rake to and fro over the surface to create a fine tilth and get rid of large lumps and stones.

1 Simple method   Broadcast the seed over the surface of the soil, then rake it in lightly.

2 More precise method   Draw shallow parallel drills over the soil surface. On average, for annual flower seeds, these should be 15cm/6in apart. As a general rule, a seed should be covered only by its own size with soil, so for fine seeds like love-in-a-mist the drills are shallow, and for larger seeds like sweet peas and French beans they are deeper.

Seedlings will need to be reduced so that the plants have room to mature (the optimum spacing is usually given on the packet). Thin mixed colours systematically rather than leaving the largest and strongest, because some colour strains are more vigorous and you might otherwise be left with just one colour.

BELOW, TOP These seedlings have been sown rather thickly and need thinning as soon as they are large enough to handle. Thin first to 2.5cm/1in, then to 8cm/3in and finally to the correct spacing (usually about 15cm/6in), as given on the seed packet.

BELOW, BOTTOM Even when sown in rows love-in-a-mist soon blends to create a lovely informal mass. Plants will seed themselves naturally after an initial introduction.

BULBS ARE AMONG THE MOST VERSATILE OF PLANTS and are of such variety that they can be added to a garden to brighten and improve borders, tubs or areas of lawn for any month of the year. Plants with similar storage organs, such as tubers and corms, are included under this heading, although botanically they are not bulbs.

Most bulbous plants are slim of habit and can be slotted in among existing plants (see pages 80–1). The two main planting times are autumn for bulbs that flower in spring (daffodils, tulips, crocus), and spring for bulbs that flower during summer and autumn (gladiolus, lilies, nerines). The main criteria for success are planting fresh, healthy bulbs and putting them in deep enough – as a rough guide cover bulbs with soil at least twice their own depth above them, but cover tulips with a good 13–15cm/5–6in of soil. Informal groupings look more effective than widely spaced or straight lines of bulbs. Some bulbs, like tulips and crocus, are even more beautiful when they open fully in the sun and so need a bright position. Others, like *Scilla mischtschenkoana*, snowdrops and daffodils, flower well in light shade and do not need direct sun. Most bulbs, but specifically alliums and lilies, need good drainage so they do not rot in winter. Daffodils, however, tend to do well in moist soils.

Tulips are ideal for a massed effect. Plant in two layers, setting the bulbs so that they do not quite touch one another. This display took about thirty bulbs in a 45cm/15in pot.

Planting bulbs into turf

Many bulbs naturalize well in grass, as long as their leaves are left unmown for at least six weeks after flowering. For large bulbs like those of daffodils and tulips, remove a small circle of turf, then plant each bulb separately. There are neat, purpose-made bulb planters for the task, which remove a core of soil wide enough to take a single bulb. The core of soil is then simply released back into the hole. To plant small and medium-sized bulbs like dwarf narcissi, however, it is easier to cut and lift a square of turf large enough to accommodate five or six bulbs, plant them and replace the turf on top.

Our crab apple, *Malus* 'Golden Hornet', is glorious with fruit in autumn and in spring narcissi brighten the area beneath it before the blossom opens. Lifting three squares of turf and planting six bulbs in each to achieve such an effect takes no more than half an hour.

What you need
- half-moon cutter, spade
- fork, trowel
- small or medium bulbs x 18

How to do it
1 Place the bulbs on the grass to decide roughly where they should grow.

2 Cut three pieces of turf 30cm/1ft square with the half moon and lift from one end with a sharp spade. Fork the soil in each patch (**A**).

3 Plant six bulbs in each square using the trowel (**B**).

4 Replace each turf carefully (**C**) and whack them hard with the flat of the spade to settle them.

Aftercare
- To help the bulbs naturalize and spread into clumps, leave the area of grass unmown until the bulb foliage has died.
- If daffodil or other bulbs grow 'blind' (do not flower) it is usually because they have grown offsets that are too crowded to reach flowering size, especially if the soil is compacted. The usual solution is to lift them just after they go dormant in late spring and divide and replant in autumn.

Bright yellow daffodil blooms on tall, slender stems look enchanting scattered through the fresh spring turf.

TIP Tiny bulbs like those of snakeshead fritillary (*Fritillaria meleagris*) can be dropped into shallow holes twice their depth made by the tines of a fork.

planting basics

27

MOST BORDER PLANTINGS INVOLVE SHRUBS and herbaceous perennials. Adding these to borders is easy, but there are one or two pitfalls to avoid. The most common reasons for plants not 'taking' are when they have been planted with dry rootballs, when pot-bound roots have not been teased out, or when the roots are either too high or too low in the ground.

Container-grown plants can be added at any time of year, although early to mid-autumn is the best time as it offers the optimum combination of cool temperatures and moist, but still warm soil. Tender shrubs, however, especially those needing good drainage, are often best left until spring.

Planting a shrub

A variegated myrtle (*Luma apiculata* 'Glanleam Gold') is an evergreen shrub just right for adding winter interest to this border. A sunny, sheltered aspect in a mild area is ideal for a plant that is only hardy to −5°C/23°F. As the myrtle grows, less permanent plants around it can be moved out of its way.

What you need
- spade, fork
- bucket of water
- soil conditioner, mulch
- container-grown shrub

How to do it
1 Check the best position for the new plant in the border (**A**).
2 Dig a hole slightly larger than the size of the shrub's container and fork plenty of soil conditioner into the bottom and into the infill soil.
3 Dunk the shrub, still in its pot, into the bucket of water and leave until no more bubbles burst to the surface (**B**).
4 Let the pot drain (**C**), then remove the plant and pick at the outside of the rootball, to tease some roots away (**D**).
5 Place the shrub in the hole, making sure it is at the correct

A

planting basics

level and that it is upright. If necessary, tilt the rootball.

6 Fill in around the roots (**E**), firming the soil with the toe of your boot, or with your hands if it is at all sticky. Water in.

7 Finish by applying a mulch (see pages 66–7) around the base of the shrub, but keep it away from the stem.

Aftercare

• Water the shrub during dry periods for at least the first summer.

TIP When planting on a slope, place a short length of plastic drainage pipe beside the shrub so that one end rests at root level and the other at soil level. Water can then be directed to the roots and will not run down the slope.

planting a tree

TREES FROM GARDEN CENTRES ARE USUALLY SOLD IN POTS and are best planted in autumn, winter or spring, when the ground is neither waterlogged nor frozen. Deciduous trees from nurseries supplied with bare roots must be planted from late autumn to spring after their leaves have fallen.

Staking trees is largely a matter of common sense. A small, young tree may need no stake at all and will probably make a stronger root system without one. Most slightly older trees benefit from a short stake for the first two to three years. With a container-grown tree, a stake should be driven in at an angle so as not to damage the rootball. A tall flimsy tree may need a taller stake – I can remember having to stake some weedy birches to the height of their crown of branches for their first six years, but they were an exception.

Planting a container-grown tree

Acer grosseri var. *hersii* is a beautifully marked snake-bark maple when grown, and gives interest all year round. Here a young tree is being planted into rough grass, so before starting it will be necessary to clear a good-sized circle of grass.

What you need
- spade, fork
- piece of plastic sheeting
- soil conditioner
- watering can
- tree stake, mallet, saw, tree tie
- container grown tree

How to do it

1 Place the sheet on the grass next to the cleared area. Dig a good-sized hole, large enough to take the roots and more, and put the soil on to the sheet.

2 Remove the tree from its pot, tease out the roots (**A**) and place in the hole.

3 Adjust the soil beneath the rootball (**B**) so that the surface will be flush with the soil surface when planting is finished, checking the level by hand (**C**).

4 Mix soil conditioner into the infill soil and push this soil in around the roots (**D**), firming with your boot.

5 Align the tree stake at an angle to the ground. Its tip should miss the rootball and it should meet the trunk

30cm/12in from the ground. In a windy garden, put it on the windward side of the tree, so the stem will be blown away from the stake.

6 Bang the stake in with a mallet and saw off any excess length.

7 Fix the trunk to the stake with a tree tie in such a way that the stake does not rub the tree (**E**).

Aftercare

• Water the young tree during droughts and keep weeds away from the base.

• If you want a clean stem, as the tree grows, gradually remove sideshoots from the lower part of the trunk.

• Inspect the tree tie regularly to make sure it is not rubbing. Do not forget to remove the stake after about three years.

TIP When a container-grown tree needs a more substantial support, drive in two upright stakes either side of the rootball and fix a horizontal pole between them, securing the tree to the pole with the tree tie.

In the absence of a proper tree tie, a length of nylon from a pair of tights does a good job, being both soft and flexible.

planting up a container

THERE IS NO POINT IN PRETENDING that growing plants in containers is low-maintenance or time-saving, but containers are worth a bit of effort as they have an instant transforming effect on a garden. And although it can be a bother to keep plants adequately watered (watering once or twice daily during hot spells), this is outweighed by how easy pots make it to grow plants in an unmessy way, without the need for clearing, digging and weeding (see also pages 108–9).

Remember that it is easier to look after a few larger pots than a vast assortment of smaller ones. Using saucers is an often made mistake, because good drainage is important and roots standing in water will suffer. The most laborious use of containers involves planting mixtures of plants in late spring for a summer display, and replacing them with a fresh set in autumn for winter and spring. It is simpler to plant single specimen plants which spend their whole lives in pots, examples being box, often as balls or other topiary shapes, dwarf pines, the Fuji cherry (*Prunus incisa* 'Kojo-no-mai'), *Acer palmatum* var. *dissectum*, *Phormium tenax* and *Rhododendron yakushimanum*. Planting acid-loving plants into pots of ericaceous (lime-free) compost enables you to grow them even if your garden soil is unsuitable.

Potting on

This Cape fig-wort (*Phygelius capensis*), bought to make a permanent container planting, will one day need an even larger pot, but it is best to increase the pot size in gradual stages. In too large a pot there is the risk that the roots will be surrounded by volumes of soggy compost which might stagnate, causing the roots to suffocate. A plant in a 15cm/6in diameter pot should be potted into a 20–25cm/8–10in pot. When the plant has filled this pot with roots pot it on again, and continue doing so until it reaches its mature size.

What you need
- frost-proof pot with drainage hole
- terracotta shards or polystyrene
- trowel
- John Innes no. 2 potting compost
- soil-less compost (e.g. coir-based compost, or pulverized bark)
- slow-release fertilizer granules
- plant to go in pot

How to do it
1 Mix the John Innes no. 2 and soil-less compost in equal quantities by volume (**A**).
2 Add a handful of the fertilizer granules (**B**).

3 Cover the drainage hole with three or four bits of crock or polystyrene (**C**).

4 Place compost over the crocks, checking that it will be the correct depth for the roots.

5 Remove the plant from its pot, gently teasing out congested roots (**D**).

6 Place the plant in its new pot, settle to the correct level and infill with compost, firming gently around the roots (**E**).

Aftercare

• Water the plant regularly.

• Even when the plant has filled the largest pot you have space for, it can grow well indefinitely, as long as it has adequate water.

• Apply slow-release fertilizer granules annually.

• If the plant looks yellow and stunted, gently scrape away as much soil as possible from the top and replace (top-dress) with new potting compost. For this, you can use John Innes no. 3, which holds a lot of fertilizer.

TIP For plants that hate waterlogging, such as *Phormium cookianum*, place a layer of expanded clay pebbles or small stones 5cm/2in deep in the bottom of the pot to filter out excess water more quickly.

APART FROM SOWING SEEDS, which is an essential gardening skill (see pages 24–5), the busy gardener may prefer to avoid plant propagation until life shifts down a gear. But making plants for free is fun and not always hugely time-consuming, and it would be silly not to take advantage of plants that virtually propagate themselves by layering or suckering or forming easily divisible clumps.

Layering is where lower stems of flexible-stemmed plants like *Euonymus fortunei* and honeysuckle sweep the ground and set root. Sever the connecting stem, and you will find that an exact replica of the parent has been created. You can start this process, usually in late winter or early spring, by selecting a long stem, making a small cut in it about 23cm/9in from the tip and pegging it down into the soil.

Propagating by transplanting suckers is more complicated, because the progeny may have originated from the roots of a stock plant which is different to the cultivar grafted above. It is best to wait until the sucker has flowered, to check its authenticity, before transplanting. *Viburnum farreri* and various chaenomeles (japonicas) sucker freely (see pages 58–9).

Splitting herbaceous plants to make more is also a form of propagation, known as division. This can be done from spring through to autumn and as well as creating new plants, it is a useful method of reinvigorating tired clumps and encouraging better flowers. Look for perennials like shasta daisies (*Leucanthemum* x *superbum*), Michaelmas daisies (*Aster novi-belgii*), pearl everlasting (*Anaphalis magaritacea*) and bergamot (*Monarda didyma*) whose loose spreading mats of roots and stems are easy to divide.

Splitting perennials

Here a group of ice plants (*Sedum spectabile*) are to be lifted in spring to create enough plants to make a border edging. They have been bulked up from one or two individuals over the last couple of years and are now ready to be divided, each into four or five new plants. The border soil into which the divided plants are to be planted should be clear of plants and weeds, and some conditioner forked into the surface. Do not add fertilizer: if over-fed, these sedums become sappy and tall and their stems will flop unattractively.

What you need
- **garden forks x 2**
- **trowel**
- **soil conditioner**
- **herbaceous perennials to be divided**

How to do it
1 Dig carefully around each plant with a fork (**A**).
2 Lift the plant and place its roots on the soil. Push the two forks into the centre of the rootball, back to back, trying to match some of the tines together. Push them right in with one foot.
3 Slowly pull the fork handles apart, together, apart again (**B**), twisting a little if necessary until the roots are prised apart with the minimum of damage.
4 If the two halves are large, repeat the process to further divide the portions, then clean up by hand into good but manageable chunks (**C**).
5 With the trowel, set the plants out along the border, about 45cm/18in apart, and plant. Firm (**D**) and water in.

TIP Large clumps of overgrown perennials with a wall of solid root are best divided by chopping with a sharp spade.

planting basics

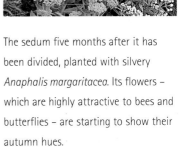

The sedum five months after it has been divided, planted with silvery *Anaphalis margaritacea*. Its flowers – which are highly attractive to bees and butterflies – are starting to show their autumn hues.

seasonal maintenance

pruning an overgrown fruit tree 38

climber control 40

pruning and tidying
clematis 42

pruning a wisteria 44

rejuvenating a rose bush 46

border care: early spring
sort-out 48

lawn care 50

border care: mid-spring
transplants 52

pond care 54

border care: staking
and propping 56

moving shrubs 58

watering and feeding 60

hedge care 62

clipping topiary 64

mulching 66

border care: summer
housekeeping 68

seed saving 70

border care: autumn tidy 72

pruning an overgrown shrub 74

the season's close 76

0

10

15

20

25

30

APPLE AND PEAR TREES GROWN IN THE GARDEN offer beauty of shape, and they provide shade, boughs for children to climb, insects for birds to feed on and, of course, fruit. Yet there are two aspects which often ruin gardeners' enjoyment of their trees: the need for spraying and pruning. However, there is an argument for not spraying (see page 159) and the pruning of home fruit trees need not be so regular, severe or structured as that for trees in commercial orchards. Just use common sense and an eye for shape. In fact, if the tree is a pleasant shape, don't bother pruning it at all. You might be surprised at how little I chose to remove from my tree in these pictures. I did not want to look at the stumpy, amputated outline that is too often the result.

Most pruning advice says that all damaged and diseased wood should be cut out. I leave a little, because I like a bit of dead wood for insects such as beetle larvae, which provide food for birds.

This apple tree was already established in the garden, but as a result of previous attempts at pruning, earlier cuts have given rise to long, upward-reaching shoots.

What you need
• pruning saw (folding)
• secateurs
• steps or a ladder (and someone to hold the ladder steady)

Starting point
Overgrown apple trees can have ugly, congested outlines but pruning during winter after leaf fall will solve the problem. Apples form on different parts of the tree according to variety, but the method below will suit all until the gardener has time to learn more.

Half-hour task
1 Where two branches are crossing and rubbing on each other, cut out the weaker one.
2 Take out any other main branches spoiling the shape of the tree, in this case just one (**A**). Weighty branches should be undercut before making the main cut, to avoid tearing bark. They can be cut back further to the main stem once the weight of the branch has been removed.
3 Reduce the length of lower branches sweeping groundwards that may obstruct a mower.
4 Where there are obvious short fruit bud-bearing spurs, trim long stems back to the last fat bud (**B**). There may be other long shoots. Cut main ones (leaders) back by three to four buds. Leave shorter sideshoots alone and trim the rest to leave four to six buds behind.

Aftercare

• The benefit of wound paint on cut surfaces is unproven, so the half-hour gardener can omit this.

• Using a 'wash' or spray to rid fruit trees of overwintering pests and their eggs not only drenches the trees in smelly spray, but robs birds (in my case a small army of blue, great, coal and long-tailed tits) of an important food source. Consider just letting nature take its course.

The pruned tree in spring; the following autumn it produced a bountiful crop of russet fruit.

climber control

TRAINING, PRUNING AND SECURING CLIMBERS go hand in hand: they are the means by which we control their growth and get the best out of them. How much and how often are dictated by how wild you like your garden to look, the space available and how rampantly the plant in question grows. Knowing when to prune is important; otherwise the constant removal of maturing wood may prevent flowering. The worst approach is that of the desperate gardener who regularly shears plants to control their growth, which results in thickets of half-dead, half-living, flowerless stems. You can get away with pruning out of season, but only by spending a few half-hours cutting here and there, thinning and shaping without removing all the wood. This way, even if both plant and its flowering season are a mystery, no harm is done.

When to prune

Winter and spring flowerers (winter jasmine, Japanese quince, early-flowering clematis) should be pruned as soon as they have finished flowering. This gives them time to grow new stems to produce flowers at the same time the following year. Climbers that flower in early summer need variable treatment, so it pays to look each one up. For example, wisteria needs a winter prune (see page 44), but mid-season clematis, such as 'Nelly Moser', are best pruned in late winter along with, but more lightly than, their late-summer-flowering cousins (see page 42). Honeysuckles are usually pruned after flowering, but I like to thin my early-flowering Dutch honeysuckle (*Lonicera periclymenum* 'Belgica') in autumn or winter, after its display of orange-red fruits. *Jasminum officinale*, which flowers in midsummer and into autumn, is best thinned after flowering. Climbing roses that start flowering in early summer and might repeat into autumn are usually pruned in late winter or, in colder regions, in spring. But I also prune in autumn to tidy up enclosed areas for the winter, with no suffering on the roses' part. Climbers which start flowering in late summer (passion flowers, Chilean potato vines) can be pruned in late winter or early spring.

Foliage climbers also have best pruning times – ivies in spring as they are coming into leaf, but Virginia creepers (*Parthenocissus*) just after their leaves have fallen. Both can be reduced during summer if their rampant stems become a nuisance.

Pruning a clematis hard back every late winter/early spring ensures that it does not swamp its host. Here a clematis climbs through a *Berberis thunbergii* f. *atropurpurea*.

What you need
- **stepladder**
- **secateurs and loppers**
- **masonry nails, hammer**
- **string or twine, bin bags**

General method for training climbers

The following applies to wall-grown or trained shrubs as well as climbers.

1 Leave attached, or tie in, a main framework of stems to fill the space offered by the wall, fence, arch or pergola. I find the simplest method of fixing stems is to tap masonry nails into the structure or wall and tie the branches to these with string or twist ties.

2 Prune away any wavy, long stems which are getting in the way or tangling around gutters. Always cut just above a node (a leaf bud or slight swelling).

3 Cut unwanted main stems close to the base of the plant.

4 Reduce the length of sideshoots growing out of main trained stems, cutting them back to spurs 5–13cm/2–5in long, depending on the scale of the plant, each containing several growth buds, which will then burst into action.

pruning and tidying clematis

CLEMATIS, POPULAR AND EASY TO INCLUDE in every garden, make excellent planting partners for climbing roses and shrubs, whether extending the season of interest or complementing the flower colour of their host. They also cause their fair share of pruning headaches.

An important point about clematis is that, given space, most will grow and flower perfectly well without pruning. The time-pressed gardener has the option of not bothering to prune them at all, though they may need some tying in to train them against pergolas and arches. But the advantages of an annual prune are better-behaved plants with healthy growth encouraged from the base.

When to prune
Early flowerers include rampant types like *Clematis montana*, which is smothered by white or pink flowers in late spring. Should they become too large, cut back from the edges after flowering until they reach manageable proportions. This method works well for all the early-flowering species.

Mid- to late-season flowerers (late spring to late summer) start producing their blooms in early summer. They can be cut back to their topmost fat pair of buds in late winter.

Late-summer flowerers can benefit from a hard pruning every late winter/early spring. The cuts can be made within 30cm/12in or so of the ground, above pairs of strong buds, but only if this has been done regularly and always into young stems. If the lower stem is old and woody at this point, prune higher up to leave short lengths of bud-bearing younger stems behind. Feed, water and mulch well for healthy regrowth.

An early performer, this *Clematis armandii* is just ending its flowering period. Now is the right moment for some light pruning and training.

seasonal maintenance

Early-flowering clematis

Clematis armandii is a vigorous, useful and pretty evergreen climber. It may eventually be necessary to prune it really hard back to get rid of dead and old stems, after which a whole rash of new stems will grow again.

Starting point

The *C. armandii* was planted in the previous season to shade an arbour. On mild spring days its fresh young growth and scented white flowers make this a favourite haven. Regular pruning and training will keep its growth within bounds.

What you need
- secateurs and loppers
- twine
- bin bags (for rubbish)

Half-hour task

1 Where strategically placed older stems have come loose from the structure and dangle, tie them in where there are gaps in leaf cover. A good method is to tie one piece of string right around the support, then secure the stem to the string (**A**).

2 In places where vigorous stems are too plentiful, unravel the growth and thin out by cutting the stems as far back as possible (**B**).

3 Having cut out plenty of old stems, train some of the young growth made this year in to replace them (**C**).

Aftercare
- Most of the new growth will cling with its own tendrils, but tie in any stems that hang low and block access.
- Apply one dressing of slow-release fertilizer in spring, and then mulch over the roots.

WISTERIAS ARE FANTASTIC PLANTS when in full flower and their foliage is pleasing, too. They can take a few years to become established, but are potentially large climbers that usually need pruning every winter.

When you buy a wisteria, opt for spending more money on a large young plant in bloom. This way, you can see that it is capable of flowering well and check that it is the sort you want. Train it in the first year (see opposite) with care: early effort pays dividends later.

Starting point

This wisteria is planted against a sunny wall and climbs up into a pergola. It has not been pruned for several years and is growing unchecked; soon, it will be twining its stems around the guttering and under roof tiles. It is really too large for the space available and will need careful pruning and training in winter every year. Pruning a large wisteria may take several sessions

What you need
• step ladder
• secateurs and loppers
• masonry nails, hammer
• string or twine, bin bags

Before pruning, this wisteria was a tangle of stems in a confined space (left). Following pruning, when unwanted stems were cut out (centre) and laterals were cut back (right), it bloomed with renewed vigour the following spring (opposite).

Half-hour task

1 Make sure older, main framework stems are tied securely to the support.

2 Some gardeners tie new stems to wires stretched against the wall, but I prefer to use either special wall-plant nails with lead hooks in them or masonry nails. Prune the ends of new stems back by one-third to help strengthen them.

3 Trace back long, unwanted older stems to their origin and cut back cleanly just above a bud, if one is visible, leaving a small peg behind.

4 On flowering plants there will be, close to the older wood, short, thick stems (spurs) holding plump, dark, dormant flower

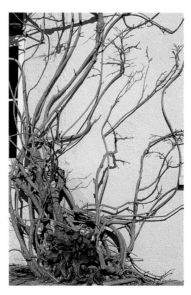

buds. These should be left.

5 Younger stems of slim growth buds extending from the flowering spurs should be shortened to two or three buds.

6 Long whippy stems growing directly out of older wood should also be shortened to two or three buds. This will help divert energy into building up flowering spurs.

Aftercare

• If the wisteria is poking you in the eye by summer, cut back waving side stems to 15cm/6in. Otherwise, save time by carrying out all the pruning in winter.

• Water wisterias during severe dry spells as they are unlikely to flower well if the roots have suffered prolonged drought.

First-year wisteria care

During the growing season, tie stems in to make a framework. The following winter, shorten these by one-third. When regrowth starts, train in the new shoots. When sideshoots not wanted for tying in grow from the main stems, prune back to 15cm/6in in summer. Reduce the trained-in laterals and leader again the following winter; then begin pruning as above.

In late winter, this rose bush has bursting and growing buds and is ready for pruning.

NEVER READ ABOUT ROSE PRUNING IN OLD GARDENING BOOKS unless you want a good laugh. Advice can run into pages and makes the process appear so complicated that it becomes intimidating. A lot of old-fashioned rose-pruning wisdom was aimed at producing a few perfect prize-winning blooms, whereas these days we want to enjoy the maximum amount of flowers over a long period.

Hybrid teas and floribundas (large-flowered and cluster-flowered roses, to give their modern terms) are what people think of as rose bushes as opposed to shrub roses or climbers (see page 73) and ramblers. Most gardens have them, though their popularity has waned. Hybrid teas tend to be a little taller than floribundas, and produce fewer, more shapely flowers per stem. Floribundas, as their name suggests, usually produce masses of flowers in large clusters.

Pruning, especially for hybrid teas, was historically severe, but the modern idea is to leave more growth on, thus increasing the foliage which fuels the plant and encouraging more flower buds. An annual pruning and feeding in late winter or early spring prevents these roses from growing straggly and helps them make plenty of flowers.

seasonal maintenance

A

B

When to prune

I time my pruning according to how much growth the plants are making. If, by late winter, their buds are really bursting and growing, I prune then. In colder regions with vicious late frosts, I would wait until early spring.

Starting point

This tall rose bush was trimmed back in autumn to tidy it and prevent wind rock; now in late winter it is ready for more extensive pruning. Keeping pruning simple should enable you to deal with at least one such rose per half hour. For very old roses with just a few thick woody stems, try sawing through one old stem per year, or keep the pruning to younger stems. As long as there is a good bush of leaves and flowers on top, bare stems below can be concealed by clever planting beneath, such as *Geranium magnificum*, foxgloves or *Artemisia* 'Powis Castle'.

What you need

- secateurs
- a stout pair of gloves
- rose fertilizer, soil conditioner
- wheelbarrow or bin bag

Half-hour task

1 Choose a point one-third to halfway up the stems of the rose and snip through all the stems at that height (**A**) with a sharp pair of secateurs. I usually make my cuts just above buds on the stem (**B**).

2 As you remove stems, place them directly into the bin bag or wheelbarrow. This saves having to handle them twice.

3 Weed beneath the bushes and sprinkle rose fertilizer over the roots (**C**).

4 Apply an 8cm/3in layer of soil conditioner as a mulch (**D**) in a 75cm/30in diameter circle around the plant, avoiding piling it around the stems.

Aftercare

- Unless you are growing a rose for attractive hips, deadhead by removing just the flower stem to keep more flowers coming,
- If you want to spray against mildew, rust or blackspot (see page 169), do so as the foliage develops, rather than waiting for symptoms to appear. Avoid spraying in sunlight, and spray again two weeks later.

After pruning, the rose is ready to make fresh foliage and flower buds.

ONE OF THE MOST SATISFYING GARDENING TASKS is to give a border a good sorting out. If you are pushed for time, just tackle a section at a time. Even sorting out an area only 2 x 1m/6 x 3ft will make a big difference, and the effect of doing sections like this when you have the chance soon adds up. One tactic is to target a section just prior to its season of glory, such as late winter or early spring to make the most of the coming spring flowers.

General tasks

1 Where there is a turf edge, re-cut if necessary using a half-moon iron (see page 51). Otherwise, trim overlong grass and push soil away from the edge to discourage grasses from rooting into the border. While working, stand on a timber footboard along the edge to avoid damaging the turf with muddy boots.

2 If a shrub has become ungainly, prune out any stems that are forming ugly thickets or encroaching on other plants (see pages 74–5).

3 Cut down any remaining dead flower stems from herbaceous perennials and remove other debris (large twigs and any dead bedding plants remaining from last year). Pull out any weeds but leave self-set seedlings. Avoid too much soil disturbance, especially around bulbs.

4 Identify gaps and spread soil conditioner as a mulch at least 5cm/2in deep over bare soil (see page 22). Plan a half-hour planting session to add new plants that will extend the season of interest.

TIP It is not too soon to plan slug control for susceptible plants like delphinium and hosta, just pushing their new shoots through the soil, with a wide barrier of sharp grit or coarse bark.

Thinning out seedlings

During spring, you may find patches of seedlings which have set all on their own. This illustrates the benefits of leaving seedheads on plants and not disturbing the soil too much. These plants, like the *Lychnis coronaria* and the honesty (*Lunaria annua*) in the picture below, are a bonus for a gardener short of time, but the results will be better for some judicious thinning and transplanting.

Use thinned seedlings to expand the patch or to make a group elsewhere. Or dibble them in here and there to create attractive interplanting effects with other plants.

seasonal maintenance

Starting point

These *Lychnis* seedlings have sown themselves in thickets among winter-flowering pansies. Thinning them out will make all the difference to their flowering performance.

It is a shame to spoil a season's display by failing to clear up just before it begins to look its best. This rather wild spring border, full of honesty and daffodils, is a delight, but only remains so because someone has come along to pull out grasses, nettles and brambles, and monitor the self-seeding of the honesty.

What you need

- small border fork
- bucket, watering can
- narrow dibber or small stick

Half-hour task

1 If the seedlings (**A**) are large enough to transplant, water the soil to moisten if necessary, and leave time for the water to soak in. Then loosen the soil lightly with the fork.

2 Gently pull out unwanted seedlings (**B**), leaving one spaced roughly every 5cm/2in.

3 Replant all or some of the seedlings you have pulled out in gaps in the border. To do this, fork over the soil, make a hole with the dibber, or a finger, insert the seedling and firm the soil around it.

4 Water the seedlings in the thinned patch (**C**) and any you have replanted.

Aftercare

- The plants may flower in their first year, but will make a better display the following year.
- Thin the seedlings again to 10–15cm/4–6in apart after they have grown on.

lawn care

THE LAWNS OF TIME-PRESSED GARDENERS have to survive without being scarified, aerated and top-dressed to within an inch of their lives. Use what time you have for the most important tasks. A lawn growing on poor soil will need feeding at least twice during a season, starting in spring. If you can't bear weeds, apply fertilizers with mosskiller and weedkiller added. Lawn fertilizers are either applied dry, as granules, or in liquid form through a watering can or hose-mounted applicator. The latter is probably best as there is less likelihood of scorching or overdosing.

At the start of a new growing season, begin mowing with the mower blades set quite high, so that the mere tips are removed. Choose dry days when the soil is not waterlogged, and continue to mow when necessary, with the blades eventually set at about 2.5cm/1in for weekly summer mowing. Alternatively, you would do well to persuade or pay someone else to mow your lawn, as it's a once a week job when the grass is growing strongly. This regularity is not for aesthetics alone, but because a lawn becomes thicker and healthier with regular cutting. Attending to bare patches and ragged edges are quick jobs that do much to improve appearance.

Repairing a bare patch

Bare patches, usually the result of wear and compaction, can quickly be made good by sowing seed in spring or autumn. Should bare patches consistently appear under trees or where lawns narrow, consider replacing the turf in these places with gravel or paving.

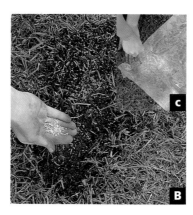

Starting point

This bare spot, caused by boisterous play, is ideal for reseeding: it is just 30cm/12in sq. Choose either coarse or fine grass seed to match with existing turf, if possible.

What you need

- lawn seed
- a little extra topsoil
- fork, rake
- square of polythene and pegs

Half-hour task

1 Fork the area thoroughly (**A**), pushing the tines in deep to loosen hard soil. Fork gently into surrounding turf, to match the level of the patch and help the repair blend in.

2 Add a little extra topsoil to the forked area and rake to and fro to get a fine, even tilth. Tread gently to settle, then rake again.

3 Sprinkle the grass seed over the bare patch (**B**) and rake it in gently.

4 Cover with polythene and peg down firmly (**C**).

Aftercare

- Remove the polythene as soon as the seed starts to germinate, or the new grass may rot.
- Let the new grass grow to 8cm/3in before its first cut.

Maintaining lawn edges

Trimming lawn edges every two to three mowings with proper edging shears will keep the lawn's definition. This may seem pernickety, but it will save time in the long run by stopping grass and lawn weeds from invading the borders. An edge left untrimmed will become ragged and need to be recut.

What you need
- half-moon cutter, fork
- wheelbarrow, to remove debris

Starting point
This lawn has been mown but its edge has been left uncut. As it is curved, it can be cut by eye, For a straight edge, set a line to show where the edge should be, measuring it in relation to other nearby lines such as walls or hedges. Lay a straight-edged board against the line, stand on the board and cut along it.

Half-hour task
1 Mark the line of the new edge on to the turf with the blade of the cutter.
2 Cut the edge by setting the curved blade in place and pushing down sharply with the foot (**A**).
3 When the edge has been cut, lift the unwanted grass out of the border with a border fork. Dense pieces of turf can be cut with the half-moon into smaller sections to make them easier to lift.

4 Fork out any weeds in the border and finish by pushing the soil away from the edge (**B**).

TIP To repair a damaged lawn edge, use the half-moon to cut a rectangle of turf containing the bare patch along one of its long sides. Slice under this with a spade, lift and turn around so that the good side becomes the lawn edge and the damamged side is inward. Fill the bare patch with topsoil and reseed if necessary.

border care: mid-spring transplants

I REPEATEDLY TELL GARDENERS THAT AUTUMN IS THE BEST TIME for moving and splitting herbaceous perennials, but the reality is that a lot of people wake up, like their gardens, in spring, and want to take action then, or find that they didn't have the opportunity to do the job in autumn. Besides which, in wet years, soils can be constantly waterlogged from mid-autumn to mid-spring, in which case leaving well alone is the best policy. In general, I prefer autumn moves because, conditions allowing, roots have a chance to start growing in moist, warm soil, which stands the plants in good for next summer, when they can be relied upon to give a more mature performance. Transplanting can be done successfully in spring but late moves carry an increased risk of hitting a dry period and will not put on as good a display as their autumn-planted counterparts.

Obvious moves include plants clearly in the wrong place. In spring, look at emerging growth and imagine the plants fully grown. It is usually easy to predict when one will swamp others, or be swamped itself. There is no harm in having taller plants dotted through the middle of a border, which avoids a contrived, tiered look, but there is no use in burying small, slender perennials right at the back. So set things right and move them into new positions.

Planting in drifts

Have you wondered how gardeners achieve that really full look in a border? They divide herbaceous perennials and grasses into small clumps, once they have bulked up sufficiently (pages 34–5), and replant them so that they merge into large flowing drifts which look great even in modest-sized gardens. They look most natural if interplanted slightly at the edges, so that one sort of plant appears to blend effortlessly with the one next to it (*Geranium endressii* with *Dicentra* 'Stuart Boothman', for instance). The plants will take a season to knit together. In the second year, further improvements can be made by dotting one sort of plant through another so that the two grow together, maximizing space and lengthening the flowering period. Bulbs like the Dutch iris opposite, daffodils and tulips can be slotted among drifts to complement their foliage and flower. Most importantly, the ground is permanently covered, which saves work.

Moving an astrantia

Here an astrantia clump is being transplanted, so as to form part of a group of astrantias to achieve a drift effect. Putting different-hued cultivars together is not a problem as they all blend together well.

What you need
- fork, spade
- soil conditioner
- watering can

Starting point

This astrantia is half-covered by shrubs which grew and spread into its space last season. In this position there will be no room for it to reach its full height of 60cm/24in and its delicate flowers will be hidden.

The plant before moving, half-hidden by previous season's growth.

seasonal maintenance

Half-hour task

1 Fork all around the roots of the astrantia, then put the tines under the plant and lift it up.

2 Identify a lightly shaded position for the plant and clear a good space of any weeds and debris growing there. Dig a generous planting hole. Add plenty of soil conditioner to the bottom of the hole and to the heap of infill soil.

3 Fork soil and conditioner together. Check the level of soil so that when the astrantia is lowered into the hole, it will be at exactly the right height (**A**).

4 Fill in around the roots, firming gently with hands or the toe of your boot. Smooth the surface over and water in generously.

Aftercare

• Water the astrantia during droughts.

• Astrantia stand well on their own, but in exposed areas push twiggy sticks in as supports.

• Where soil is poor, a sprinkling of general-purpose fertilizer around the plant after planting will work wonders.

TIP Large, matted clumps of perennials in heavy soil may put up a struggle when moved. Using a sharp spade, dig around them to gain access, chopping them in bits if necessary. They will not take harm and can be tidied up afterwards.

The transplanted *Astrantia major* 'Hadspen Blood' takes its place with pink and white forms in a drift of astrantias with iris in the foreground.

pond care

GARDEN PONDS NEED ROUTINE MAINTENANCE just as much as beds and borders. Every spring the more rampant plants, such as water irises and rushes, will need curbing by splitting and repotting. Water lilies need similar attention every few years, according to their size and vigour. By spending regular half-hours on pond maintenance – see opposite – it should be possible to avoid the arduous and time-consuming task of completely emptying, cleaning and refilling the pond, which upsets its natural balance.

Should a pond become filthy and stagnant, it might be because it has insufficient plant life or too many fish fouling the water. In this case, it is best to clean it out and start again with a better balance of plants (see page 92), fewer fish or a filter to cleanse the water. Late spring is the best time for this, as most tadpoles have already changed into frogs, and the pond has the rest of summer in which to recover.

Dividing water lilies
Use this method for marginal aquatics that are standing in pots or rooted in the soil in shallow water, as well as for water lilies.

What you need
- secateurs
- old, serrated carving knife
- aquatic plant basket(s)
- hessian for lining
- aquatic plant compost or good garden soil
- shingle or gravel, for mulching baskets
- wheelbarrow to remove debris

Starting point
In this pond the water lilies, already coming into growth, have outgrown their container and are threatening to swamp their corner. Repot in shade to avoid scorching the young leaves, and do not add fertilizer.

Half-hour task
1 Haul the water lilies from the pond and with the carving knife cut the rootstock into manageable portions. Then with secateurs cut fresh chunks with healthy growing points to fit the new baskets (**A**).
2 Line the baskets with hessian, then repot the fresh pieces into compost or soil (**B**).
3 Top the surface off with the shingle and gently ease the container back into the water. Water depth for lilies varies from 15cm/6in to 2m/6ft, according to their ultimate size, so check them individually.

Aftercare
• Do prevent other pond plants from invading the water lilies.
• Do not combine vigorous fountains with water lilies since lilies dislike turbulent water.

TIP Most marginals will be happy if the surface of their pot is covered by 5cm/2in or so of water.

Seasonal care

Spring Lift, divide and replace marginals and lilies just as they come into growth to restrict size. Add new plants if necessary. If the pond is full of leaves, dredge small areas at a time, putting leaves and dead plant material around the pond sides for creatures like fresh water shrimps, dragonfly larvae and newts. Clean the pond out now, if it is essential.

Summer Remove excess oxygenating weed regularly, and also strands of blanket weed by twirling with a stick. Net off unwanted duck weed. A sudden increase in warmth and sunlight may cause algal growth to turn the water a soupy green. This should only be a temporary nuisance. Make sure there is enough oxygenating weed, and add more plants with floating leaves to shade the water. If the situation is bad, install a pump and filter. Top up with water to compensate for evaporation.

Autumn Trim submerged dead foliage from pond plants. Place netting over the pond to catch falling leaves, using bricks or pegs to weigh it down. If there are many trees in the vicinity, the net may need emptying before the leaves become too sodden. Putting a double net on so that one stays in place when the top one is removed is helpful.

Winter A ball or other floating object will help prevent freezing. Fish and pond life can suffer without air, so create breathing holes in ice by melting it (a pan of boiling water does the trick). Never hit ice as this sends shock waves through the water.

Twirling pond weed out with a stick is something that can be done in leisurely fashion whenever you have a few minutes to spare. Choose a fairly stout stick – otherwise the weight of weed will break it.

By midsummer, pond weed growth is fantastic and needs to be controlled. This degree of intermingling, with submerged weed growing up through the water, is acceptable, as long as it is prevented from choking the lilies.

THERE ARE FEW SIGHTS MORE GORGEOUS than full, billowing summer borders, but tall, floppy stems easily fall prey to heavy rainstorms, which can flatten them and spoil a border overnight. If you are pushed for time you would be wise to avoid the taller herbaceous perennials, but if you have inherited some, you will need to give them support.

My favourite supports are twiggy sticks 60–120cm/12–48in long gathered from beech, hazel, birch or elm suckers, shrub prunings or hedge cuttings (garden centres sell them as pea sticks). Cut the bases at an angle so that the sticks can easily be pushed into the soil, tie in bundles and store until needed. Used as supports around the thrusting stems of herbaceous perennials, they are natural-looking and effective. A couple of sticks can be added later in the season where escaped stems have sprawled out. Garden centres also sell purpose-made supports. Some fix together around a plant, others are pushed in above the emerging plant to make a grid of cane or plastic-coated wire through which the plant stems grow (see below). There are also flexible metal supports that can be linked together in sections to produce any size or shape. They may be unsightly to begin with, but will soon be obscured by growth.

Wigwams, created from willow or hazel, and ornate metalwork obelisks are useful as plant supports, and can be decorative in their own right (see page 8 and page 107). Use them to add dramatic height as well as support. I try to avoid bamboo canes and string because they are so straight, hard to disguise and, without effective capping, a danger to eyes.

Ideally, supports should be in place before they are needed, so that stems can grow through them and withstand summer rain and wind.

Propping up a campanula

Campanula lactiflora 'Loddon Anna', a classic of the herbaceous border, has long flowering stems that can fall about after summer squalls. Flailing stems sprawling across other plants can ruin a good piece of planting, but apply any remedial action sensitively. Simply bunching stems together and tying them to a cane can look worse than leaving them flopping about and loose.

Starting point

Not having been supported at the correct time in spring, the campanula has been beaten about by rain. All is not lost: twiggy sticks provide the answer.

What you need

• **sheaf of long twiggy sticks, their bases cut to a point**
• **border fork**
• **secateurs, pocket knife, string**

Half-hour task

1 Wade into the border armed with a few long sticks and collect up one or two stems, raising them to an upright, but natural-looking position. Insert a stick or two into the soil so that the stems are supported.

2 Continue around the plant,

seasonal maintenance

repeating this process until all the stems are supported.

3 If a stick cannot be easily pushed into the soil, cut the end to a sharper point and fork the soil to loosen it. Secure sticks with string if necessary.

4 Check that the stems look natural, and fork the soil to remove footprints as you retreat.

TIP For a more sophisticated look, bend and tie in tops of supporting sticks together over the plants when young. The rustic crabpot effect is worth the extra time.

ABOVE This *Campanula lactiflora* 'Loddon Anna' (left) has taken a tumble. The solution is to insert sticks to support the stems (right).

BELOW The campanula is now upright, the sticks all but disguised, next to **Verbascum chaixii** with red-leaved *Fuchsia magellanica* var. *gracilis* 'Tricolor' in the foreground.

This chaenomeles is forming a thicket of suckers and it is now the time to take action, to bring the shrub back to one main plant.

Transplanting a sucker

Take advantage of the many shrubs which reproduce themselves by sending up suckers (exact replicas of themselves) or by making natural layers (stems rooting where they sweep the ground (see page 34)). If left, the original plant will form a great thicket, but by lifting and transplanting the suckers or layers, you can create new individuals and keep the old plant to a sensible size.

LONG-LIVED SHRUBS NEED SPACE TO MATURE and reach their full potential. Even expert gardeners have trouble planting new shrubs in the right position and need to move at least a few. The correct approach is to space them according to eventual size and fill the gaps between with smaller shrubs and perennials. But it is always tempting to plant them too close together. Another good reason to move shrubs is changing one's mind. I often decide that a shrub I planted two years ago would look better somewhere else. Also, no two gardeners plan alike and if you move house you might not approve of the previous owner's planting. Fortunately most shrubs take little harm by being transplanted, as long as care is taken. Move them further apart while young, during their first three or four years.

Autumn is a good time for transplanting because the still warm, moist soil will encourage new roots to grow quickly. The plant can settle in before the cold of winter and put down roots before summer droughts. Deciduous shrubs must be moved while their leaves are off, so transplant them any time between autumn and spring as long as the soil is neither frozen nor waterlogged.

A

Starting point

A chaenomeles is obscuring a window and after flowering will be pruned. Some stems can be cut right back, others shortened and sideshoots pruned to 13cm/5in. One of its suckers is to be transplanted into a new border.

What you need

- spade and fork
- loppers
- some hessian
- bucket of well-rotted compost, or soil conditioner and some slow-release fertilizer

Half-hour task

1 Dig a trench all around the sucker to be transplanted, about 30cm/12in away from its trunk and a spade deep.
2 Sever small roots with the spade. Cut tougher roots and the connection between the parent and sucker with the loppers (**A**). Compacted soil can be loosened with the fork.
3 Slide the spade under the roots and cut all round the sucker (**B**).
4 Rock the plant to and fro to break any remaining roots and cut away any stubborn ones.
5 Lift the sucker carefully. Should the rootball show signs of breaking up, slide hessian beneath it and wrap it to hold it together with its soil.
6 Dig a hole larger than the rootball, fork the soil underneath and work in some of the fertilizer and conditioner. Add the rest to the infill soil.
7 Place the rootball in the hole, making sure that the soil mark on the trunk is at the surface when planting is finished (**C**).
8 Fill in carefully, firming the soil gently with the toe of your boot as you go.

The offspring sitting happily in its new border home. It could now be underplanted with bulbs followed by hardy geraniums or pulmonarias.

9 Don't forget to go back to the old site and fill in the hole.

Aftercare

- While the moved shrub is developing strong new roots, it is important to keep it watered during the first summer.
- After flowering, prune the sucker's sideshoots to 13cm/5in.

TIP When moving an evergreen shrub to an exposed site, put up a windbreak (made of woven hazel or plastic windbreak material, supplied by garden centres) on the windward side to help prevent the wind from rocking roots and dragging moisture from the foliage.

WATERING, AND IN PARTICULAR, FEEDING PLANTS can easily become complicated matters, but if you treat your soil well, adding plenty of organic matter as mulch (see page 22 and page 66) at planting times, you will minimize the occasions when you need to step in with food and water. Be guided by common sense. Too much watering can be counter-productive, as it tends to bring roots up to the surface and discourages them from growing deep down in search of moisture. Plants then become increasingly reliant on artificial watering. Over-enthusiastic applications of fertilizer can cause too much sappy growth, creating plants that need ever more support, or are more vulnerable to winter frost.

Fertilizer content varies. Nitrogen encourages leafy growth and phosphate healthy roots. Potassium helps plants bloom and set fruit, and also hardens growth for winter. Choose fertilizer with appropriate levels for your needs. Trace elements necessary for growth are often included (see page 160), and the packaging usually makes clear what the product is aimed at (acid-loving shrubs, tomatoes, etc.). Note that strong plants with vigorous roots benefit more from fertilizers than sickly plants that are less able to take up the feed. Application method varies also.

How to apply fertilizer
Slow-release fertilizers Usually as granules to the soil around the roots. These release their contents gradually over time.
Dry fertilizers As granules or powder when the soil is moist but not saturated. Avoid contact with foliage. These act more instantly.
Liquid fertilizers Dilute with water and apply under the leaves and over the roots, which absorb them quickly.
Foliar feeds Dilute then spray or water on to the plant's foliage. To avoid scorch, do not apply when the sun is shining.

Seasonal applications
Late winter/early spring On thin, poor soils, give a dressing of slow-release fertilizer to trees, shrubs, roses, clematis and similar container-grown plants, and cover with a mulch. This will last the plants all season.

The best way to water or give a liquid feed is directly on to the soil under the foliage, in the cool of evening or early morning. This avoids evaporation.

seasonal maintenance

Late spring Where soils are poor, add fertilizer (such as pelleted chicken manure) to crops and bedding at planting time or as the crop develops.

Early summer Give a liquid feed to bedding plants (rudbeckias, impatiens) or crops (tomatoes, courgettes). Use a high-potassium type for fruiting plants and a general-purpose type for flowers.

Mid- to late summer Some shrubs (camellia, rhododendron, witch hazel and wisteria) begin to set buds now for the following year. Water them generously during dry periods to safeguard their flowering potential.

Half-hour routine for high summer

Containers are likely to need a daily watering now even if it rains, because of the thick canopy of foliage and flowers covering the pot. Those with bedding plants will need weekly liquid feeds (unless they contain slow-release fertilizer). Note that watering routines will vary throughout the growing season and according to what is being grown; watch out also for rain shadows cast by walls, fences and buildings. A watering and feeding routine should be a pleasant half-hour when you take the opportunity to reflect on the beauty and productivity of the plants. For greater efficiency, follow the same route each time. Return the cans to the same point and coil or rewind hosepipes on to their reels. The half-hour gardener has no time to waste chasing lost cans and unknotting hosepipes.

What you need
- watering cans, hosepipe
- general-purpose liquid fertilizer

Half-hour task

1 Check pots first, to see if any need water. On a feed day, put fertilizer in the can and add water to mix. Ensure all the roots receive their fair share.

2 If the weather is dry, move on to crops. Watering into small depressions helps water soak in around the roots.

3 During droughts, water trees and shrubs that were planted or transplanted during the previous autumn to spring.

4 Water herbaceous perennials that were split and replanted in spring, as their roots will not be deep enough to withstand drought. Look around for and water any other plants showing signs of stress, with wilting leaves or drooping flowers.

TIPS Acid-loving plants (pieris, rhododendron, camellia) need rainwater (if hard), so collect and store this in a water butt. Ailing plants with sick roots are unable to take fertilizer up, but may respond to a foliar feed.

seasonal maintenance

hedge care

HEDGES CAN BE MOST ATTRACTIVE AND EFFECTIVE garden barriers, although they need more maintenance than a fence or wall. Noise, wind and dust are filtered by twigs and leaves and birds will be encouraged to the garden by an on-site haven for roosting and nesting. All hedges need regular upkeep but, like lawn-mowing, hedge-trimming is a job you might persuade someone else to do without losing artistic control of the garden. They should be cut so that they taper in slightly at the top. This strengthens them, allows light to reach all the shoot tips and helps them resist wind and snow.

To plant a hedge, mark its line with a string first and condition the soil really well. Most deciduous hedge plants benefit from early training. Just prune back long stems by one-third at planting time or in spring: this encourages branching and thickens them up. With evergreens, prune the sides but leave the leader.

Beech (*Fagus sylvatica*) is my favourite low-maintenance hedge. It can be cut and kept at anywhere between 1.2m/4ft and 6m/20ft high. Its leaves turn russet and cling on during winter, and it needs only an annual cut (during late summer). Evergreens requiring a once-a-year cut are glossy laurel (clip with secateurs) and spiny *Berberis* x *stenophylla,* which will deter intruders. Trim berberis after flowering and also *Osmanthus* x *burkwoodii*, a deep green evergreen smothered in small white, fragrant flowers in spring.

Probably the classiest evergreen hedge is yew (*Taxus baccata*), giving a smooth, dark backdrop between 1.2m/4ft and 3.7m/12ft high. Yew should ideally be trimmed twice, in summer and autumn. For a classic small evergreen hedge, box (*Buxus sempervirens*) is a favourite, but it needs clipping three times a year for a good, close finish. So too does Leyland cypress (x *Cupressocyparis leylandii*), which, despite its bad press, can make a neat hedge quickly.

Lavender (see pages 110–11) and rosemary make delightful low, aromatic hedges, while a large garden can play host to a rose hedge of fragrant *Rosa rugosa* which sets goblet-shaped hips after its deep pink flowers. One of the most satisfying informal hedges is a mixture of plants like sloe, hawthorn, hazel, holly, field maple and beech. Add the odd elder and wayfaring tree (*Viburnum lantana*) for punctuation, and you recreate a country hedgerow that is ideal for wildlife, too.

Half-hour hedge trim

For a short stretch of hedge like this yew (opposite) I usually clip by eye, but for longer lengths of hedge fix a line across the top to be sure of a straight finish. For large hedges, by all means use a powered cutter, but always use a residual current device and be aware of the cable.

Starting point

This yew hedge has been left to grow all season and is only now in late summer being clipped for the first (and last) time this year. A single cut saves time, but the finish of the hedge will be less dense, the work more strenuous and there will be many more clippings to collect in one go.

What you need

- shears, rake, garden steps
- sheeting to catch clippings
- wheelbarrow or rubbish bags

Half-hour task

1 Clear weeds and debris from around the base of the hedge. If space allows, spread the sheeting on the ground.

2 Begin to clip off most of this season's growth, starting at the sides (**A**). Stop frequently to gauge the smoothness of the slope, which should taper in towards the top. Empty the sheet.

3 Having cut a significant area, tackle the top on the same side (**B**), climbing on to steps if necessary. Continue clipping, but stop to check the shape periodically.

4 There may be the odd bulge where older growth has been left after previous clippings. Yew will sprout from its old stems, so it is possible to cut into these with secateurs or loppers to improve shape.

5 Make a final emptying of the sheeting and rake up any clippings that have scattered.

Here shaped plants help to create symmetry and a strong framework in a corner of a large garden, making a beautiful vista which could just as easily take place in a small garden. Sloping the hedge ends makes this part of the garden appear wider than it really is. The shaping can be achieved either by early training or by cutting into a mature hedge. Note the paired mophead trees and plantings of purple catmint, as well as the foreground potentillas which lend their support to yet soften the formal touch.

SOLID SCULPTURAL SHAPES, whether walls, pillars, ornaments, trees or topiary, are valuable assets to the garden. They are props against which a flowing mass of shrubs and herbaceous plants works well. Take a critical look at your garden and imagine what the effect of some shaped plants would be. It might be enhanced, for example, by a hedge. Hedge tops are straightforward to cut, and even an established hedge can be encouraged to grow taller and be given a sloped, pointed or scalloped top. Some hedges respond well to being cut into (beech, hornbeam, box, yew) but others do not (the *Cupressus* and *Cupressocyparis* tribe, e.g. Leyland cypress).

Topiary, another way of shaping plants, seems to work best in simpler forms. Bay pyramids spaced throughout a garden can tie in unruly planting. Box spirals and balls in containers can be moved around to create different scenes. But a word of warning: shrubs like bay and box cannot tolerate being dry at the roots and a plant will soon deteriorate if watering is not up to scratch. Ready-shaped plants are expensive, which reflects the length of time spent on them in the nursery compared to other shrubs. Growing your own is time-consuming, but satisfying. For anything but the simplest shapes push a frame around the plant to act as a guide. For a box spiral, grow a pyramid or tall cone first, then cut the pyramid into a spiral shape.

Box balls are at their prettiest in spring when fresh growth bursts from dark green foliage. But to keep a tight, well-filled shape, most of the new growth needs trimming before it grows too long, which helps keep a good appearance through the summer.

Care of box balls

During winter and early spring, the bare appearance of this terrace arbour is offset by a pairing of evergreen box balls, moved in from another part of the garden.

To start off a box ball, let a young plant grow loosely into shape, and then nip back long shoots so that they branch and are encouraged to fill out into any large spaces.

A

B

Starting point

As new growth gets under way on this box ball (**A**), it is time to clip it so as to correct its shape and ensure the plant keeps a tight outline.

What you need

- sharp, lightweight shears
- broom, dustpan, rubbish bag

Half-hour task

1 Begin clipping, tackling the sides and top, so that most of the regrowth disappears (**B**).

2 Step back frequently to make sure a spherical shape is being maintained (**c**).

3 Correct anomalies in shape by cutting harder into the stems if necessary. Sweep up.

Aftercare

- Treat the box plant to a dressing of slow-release fertilizer, applied to the soil in the top of the pot. If compost has eroded, add a little more to keep the roots well covered.
- Make sure potted plants are checked and watered regularly, especially if standing in full sun. Pot-bound plants which dry out quickly will fare better if moved into a position of light shade.
- Straggly or neglected box can be cut back really hard; the regrowth will be easier to train.

Though drastic, a hard cut makes a tight shape. New growth will fill it out in a couple of weeks.

C

mulching

BARE EARTH IN BEDS AND BORDERS IS A LIABILITY, as it is vulnerable to drying out, is available for weeds and presents an open invitation to cats and foxes. Spreading a layer of mulch over the surface between plants supresses weeds and locks moisture into the soil beneath. Mulches should therefore always be applied to moist soil, never to dry.

Coarse shingle makes a great mulching material, because water always collects under stones but weeds find it difficult to penetrate. 'Fun' materials, ranging from coloured glass chippings, dyed wood shreddings, white or coloured stones, seashells or even pine cones are popular and present more of a barrier to weeds.

Types of mulch

Soil conditioners Garden compost, leaf mould, well-rotted manure, mushroom compost and composted bark (see page 22) are all suitable as mulch and add nutrients to the soil. But take care: some may contain weed seeds which then germinate and defeat the object.

Cocoa shell A light, easy-to-handle mulch that smells faintly of chocolate. As it breaks down, a mould appears during warm, moist weather, which, though harmless, is not to everyone's liking.

Bark This robs the soil of nutrients, so a slow-release fertilizer should be added to the soil first. Chips or chunks of bark, besides appearing too 'commercial', tend to drift on to paths and lawns.

Cockle or other shells They can be pretty, but a challenge to track down in quantity, so use for pots. They may smell fishy for a while.

Pine cones These are free and effective and easy to come by, but do not last long before rotting down. Also, like bark, they may cause nutrient deficiencies. When they become too old, put them in a heap with pine needles to break down into an acidifying soil conditioner.

Shingle Larger-sized stones make an effective, stable mulch. Fine shingle is a nuisance when it sticks to feet and then falls off on to lawns and paths, and seeds of both plants and weeds can germinate in it, which can be either desirable or undesirable.

Woven membrane Spread like a carpet, this is an effective weed suppressor. Time spent laying it reaps dividends in easy care later. Cut holes for planting spaces, and a thick mulch of bark or shingle will mask the material. However, I prefer to have access to my soil.

ABOVE, TOP Here pine cones are used as an attractive mulch set against a planting of common toadflax (*Linaria vulgaris*), a wildflower that self-seeds to make a good garden plant.

ABOVE, BOTTOM Grasses in a 'dry' beach-style garden created with a shingle mulch.

seasonal maintenance

Mulching with shingle

Raised beds are prone to drying out, so taking steps to conserve moisture saves time and protects plants from stress, particularly if the bed is in a windswept, sun-baked position. When you plant, set rootballs 2.5–5cm/1–2in higher than usual, so that the plants will not be swamped by stones. Even near the seaside you must buy your own stones for their removal is prohibited from most beaches.

Starting point

The beds in this seaside garden need a shingle mulch to protect them from the effects of wind and sun. The addition of different-sized stones will give variety to the textures.

What you need

- 1 x 25kg/55lb bag of 25mm/1in shingle per sq.m/yd of soil
- random larger pebbles

Half-hour task

1 Start with the small-grade shingle, using both hands to scoop it up. Feed the stones around the plants 8cm/3in thick, ensuring that the foliage is kept clear of the mulch.
2 Scatter the larger stones amongst the shingle, but make sure the entire mulch is not deeper than 8cm/3in.

Aftercare

- New plants will need to be watered during their first growing season, but thereafter they should be self-supporting.
- If you need to replace a plant, scrape the shingle away, uproot the casualty, and replace with a new plant from another plant family. Replace the stones.

In this small seaside garden, various drought-tolerant plants including lavenders, New Zealand flax and *Lotus hirsutus* are thriving in raised boundary beds with the help of a shingle mulch. Few weeds will be able to germinate in the shingle. In the triangular bed in the foreground, a random collection of pebbles has been used as a mulch for a new planting.

MIDSUMMER IS THE TIME TO PAY ATTENTION TO BORDERS which have looked good in spring and early summer but need help to extend their performance into late summer and autumn. This is particularly so in small gardens, where every patch of ground has to work hard. Late summer can be a difficult time in the garden, as many plants will have finished their main performance and the season is usually dry.

Take a good look at the whole border to gain an overview of what needs attention, then home in on small sections at a time. Apart from cutting back and tidying up, gap-filling with a few new plants for instant colour will make all the difference. Summer garden shows are good places to find perennials like penstemons, which settle in well as long as they are adequately watered. Garden centres stock bedding-type plants, grown on in larger pots, with potential to flower into autumn. Look for different kinds of rudbeckia or dianthus to group informally, or lilies and lavenders, which will keep going from year to year. When plants are close to their flowering season it may not be the best time for them to establish, but buying them then does make it easier to find good performers.

Starting point

The aim is to prolong the flowering season of this border. Geraniums are worth deadheading, as some flower again, *Geranium* 'Johnson's Blue' for instance flowering on into autumn. When the euphorbias lose their freshness, cut their tall flower heads back and they will refurbish themselves (but wear gloves to protect skin from irritant sap). Some faded flowers should be left, such as the purple allium globes, as they bear attractive seedheads. Small changes in autumn would make care of the border easier, perhaps moving the wispy golden grass in the foreground and filling the gap with more of the variegated astrantia, geraniums, *Helleborus foetidus* Wester Flisk Group, *Vinca difformis*, bugles or bergenias.

What you need
- wheelbarrow, loaded with:
- border fork, spade
- secateurs, loppers
- gloves
- soil conditioner
- watering can

Half-hour task

1 Clean through the border sensitively, removing weeds and dead material, but avoid taking out too much.

2 Deadhead plants like hardy geraniums which may flower again, leaving some to set seed.

3 Prune any shrubs that have just finished flowering, such as deutzia and philadelphus, and clip topiarized plants such as box or *Lonicera nitida*.

4 Into gaps where flowering plants have dwindled, fork in soil conditioner, then replant with bought-in rudbeckias or a pot of fresh lilies. Water in.

5 During prolonged droughts, give any wilting plants a full can of water to their roots.

With a bed at its peak it is easy to feel complacent, but all too soon it could become a muddle. Here when the clumps of blue *Geranium x magnificum* stop flowering, biennials like the blue-spired *Anchusa azurea* 'Loddon Royalist' fade, and the mound of *Lonicera nitida* 'Baggesen's Gold' grows stragglier, some tidying up will help the bed look good into autumn.

seed saving

IT CAN BE TEMPTING TO FILL EVERY SPARE HALF-HOUR in the garden with physical labour. But just wandering about need not be a dreadful waste of time: it is an opportunity for a valuable inspection. Another excellent way to enjoy the garden without too much exertion is to gather something from it.

Midsummer to autumn sees a rash of seed capsules and pods ripening under the hot sun and it is worth saving the seeds of favourite plants. Well-labelled seeds from the garden also make great presents for other gardeners. As with all aspects of gardening, observation is the key. Watch as flower petals fall and firm greenish pods or fruits develop. As the pods age and dry, the seeds inside change from green or white to hard grey, brown or black. Seed collection must then take place quickly, before the plant's dispersal mechanism kicks in. Some are surprisingly violent, with pods bursting and flinging out their contents. Others dehisce placidly, dropping their seed close by.

In this delightful mingling of flowers and seedheads, opium poppies (*Papaver somniferum*) sown into gaps provide not only silky petals, but structural, glaucous pods. These green poppy pods are not yet ripe. Once they have ripened and dried out, the seeds rattle inside and holes appear in the top of the pods.

Poppy seeds can be shaken from their pods easily, into a paper bag. To maintain a particular flower colour, remove plants with flowers of less desirable hues as soon as they open the following year.

Starting point

The drying flower heads of this *Salvia forsskaolii* are ready to be collected by snipping off the stem into a labelled bag. Later, they can be separated from their capsules and dealt with (see below). Like all seed collection, the task needs to be done on a dry, sunny day.

What you need

- scissors or secateurs
- paper bags, plastic film canisters
- envelopes, pencil

Half-hour task

1 Write each plant name and the date on separate paper bags.
2 Snip off whole seedheads straight into the paper bags (**A**).
3 Spread the stems or heads out on a sunny windowsill or dry place away from draught and they will dry out perfectly.

Aftercare

- Sit down with the dried heads and patiently remove the seeds from their nut-like capsules.
- Place seeds in a smaller, labelled envelope or plastic film container.
- Store the seeds in a cool, dry, frost-free place.

Rowan (*Sorbus*) seeds can be squashed from their berries straight into a pot. Cover lightly with compost and a thin layer of sharp grit, and leave outdoors all winter; they need to feel the cold to germinate.

When to sow your seeds

Hardy annuals (nigella, poppy), biennials (foxgloves) and smaller perennials (aquilegias, *Salvia forsskaolii, Lychnis coronaria*): sow straight into the soil or into pots left outdoors or in a cool place during autumn or spring.
Half-hardy annuals (most bedding plants such as petunias, impatiens): for a good start sow inside, in warmth, during spring.
Herbaceous perennials and hardy shrubs: sow in autumn when fresh then leave outdoors, protected from rodents, to feel the cold as they would naturally. Most will germinate the following spring, though some take eighteen months.

seasonal maintenance

THE AIM OF AN AUTUMN TIDY is definitely not to 'put the garden to bed', for this would waste an entire six months of autumnal and wintry excitements. But by mid-autumn, most annuals and tender perennials will look wretched enough to put on the compost heap. Clearing them will allow autumn tints to come into their own uncluttered.

A typical border tidy means weeding, removal of leaves and cutting back of sprawling, unwanted dead stems (but leave attractive ones). Where large gaps of soil are uncovered, try to find time to plant them up. Especially in areas of high rainfall, it is better not to leave soil exposed and prone to waterlogging. Mid-autumn is an ideal time for planting shrubs, herbaceous perennials and bulbs.

Regardless of correct timing, you can do some necessary pruning such as thinning thickets of stems and cutting out stems invading paths or other plants' territories.

Once the leaves of dahlias and cannas are blackened, decisions need to be made. Half-hour gardeners in mild regions can leave the tubers to overwinter without disturbance. Where frost habitually penetrates the ground deeply, they are best lifted (see page 127).

Make sure glowing autumnal scenes can be properly enjoyed: a clean-out of summer-planted annuals, weeds and dead stems will allow the colourful leaves of viburnums, stems of dogwoods and berries of cotoneaster to shine uncluttered.

Tidying up a climbing rose

Most gardens have a few climbing roses for which the textbook pruning time is spring. However, in small spaces, an autumn pruning and tying in neatens the garden for winter and works well for the rose in all but the coldest areas, where hard frosts can cause dieback. If you don't have time to prune one year, try at least to tie in any long stems that obscure doorways and paths. They will produce the most flowers if tied in horizontally, so that sap can flow evenly along the length and not push its power up to the top of the stem.

Starting point

During spring this rose 'Climbing Etoile de Hollande' was pruned and tied in. First, a couple of the oldest stems were cut right back to allow healthy new ones to grow. Some stems were tied in to make a framework and their sideshoots were shortened by two-thirds. But as the rose shares its space with a honeysuckle and wisteria, space is at a premium and by autumn, waving stems are blocking the passageway. A good tidy-up now should solve this.

What you need

- secateurs and loppers
- thick gloves (if rose is thorny)
- string, bin bags (for rubbish)

Half-hour task

1 Check ties on the main framework of stems and retie or replace as necessary (no older stems will need removing as this was done in spring). Tie in any new stems to fill gaps.

2 Cut away any unsightly dead or weak stems.

3 Cut off the tips of long stems where they have outgrown their support.

4 Cut back any sideshoots that have finished flowering by a good two-thirds (**A**).

Aftercare

- The rose may need a light pruning at the usual time in spring. If any of the stems have died back, they can be trimmed by cutting above the last healthy bud.
- In spring, clear weeds from around the base, and apply rose fertilizer if the soil is poor and to improve soil condition.
- To help retain moisture, spread an 8cm/3in mulch of well-rotted compost or other soil conditioner around the root area.

Summer deadheading of this rose has brought late blooms mingling with honeysuckle fruits.

Ablaze with autumn colour, this *Cotoneaster simonsii* has way outgrown its allotted space.

THE PROBLEM WITH MOST PRUNING INSTRUCTIONS is the assumption that gardeners know the name and growing habits of all their plants. The reality is that many people inherit a thicket of mixed shrubs and have no idea what they are, so talking to a new gardener about current and previous season's woody growth has him or her glazing over as fast as I do when confronted by a computer expert.

Although it is still a good plan to prune during the correct season if you know it, the alternative is a method that suits virtually any shrub and which can be carried out at almost any time of year.

A

Starting point

This technique can be applied to any shrub that has become ugly and outgrown its position, is invading the growing spaces of other shrubs, shading out choice plants or blocking a view. This autumn-fruiting *Cotoneaster simonsii* forms part of a boundary hedge that has grown too large and is annoying the neighbours. Its textbook pruning time is after flowering in early summer, but I tackled it in early autumn.

The object is to thin out about one-third of the stems, so that the shrub becomes shorter and less congested. Leaving two-thirds of the stems in place means that blooms will still open next summer.

What you need

- pruning saw or loppers
- secateurs (for stems less than 1cm/½in diameter)
- rubbish bags

Half-hour task

1 Walk around the shrub, noting particularly any thickly congested branches or badly misshapen areas. Use common sense when pruning, keeping the plant's natural proportions in mind (see page 144).
2 Target an older stem (**A**), and cut it out, close to the base, side branches and all, using the pruning saw or loppers. If, however, the stem bears a promising-looking bud or side growth heading in the right direction to fill a gap, do not cut near the base but cut above the side growth (**B**). Where possible cut above a node, denoted on older stems by a slight swelling or a ring.
3 Repeat until about one-third of the stems have gone and the shrub looks more relaxed (**C**).
4 Use the secateurs to tidy up any thin, twiggy growths that spoil the overall shape or may cause obstructions. Avoid the urge to trim the plant all over, as this will remove too many berried shoots, spoil the shape and result in thicket-like regrowth. Leaving two-thirds of the stems in place means that blooms will still open next summer.

B

C

As AUTUMN FADES INTO WINTER, once the leaves of deciduous plants have fallen, the garden is stripped back to its bones. Careful pruning of deciduous shrubs will have left twiggy, yet not invasive outlines, while interesting seedheads can be left for structure, hibernating insects and natural bird food. Now the importance of planting some evergreens for year-round structure, and maintaining shapes such as turf edges, as well as keeping hedges and topiary clipped, becomes clear.

Even in the depths of winter, it is important to refresh the spirit by getting outdoors for the odd half-hour when weather allows. When the soil is neither waterlogged nor frozen, it is still possible to plant trees, as well as shrubs and herbaceous perennials. Garden centres are stocked with an inspiring range of evergreens and winter-flowering treasures such as viburnums, mahonias, winter jasmine and winter honeysuckle, which tend to be overlooked at other times of the year.

The advantage of maintaining the garden in short sessions throughout the growing season is that by winter you will need to do no more than give the garden a little general care.

Stems of cranesbills caught in low shafts of wintry light are bound together by the intrictate workmanship of a gingery orb-web spider.

General care

1 Autumn leaves are so beautiful that it is a shame to rush out and clear them all up. But do not let soggy leaves lie on lawns or on top of delicate plants for too long. Lift them from heavily planted areas to make leaf mould, but in wilder, out-of-the-way places between shrubs they can be left to rot down naturally, which saves time.

2 Turf edges are particularly vulnerable to damage from feet during winter and it is a good idea to lay boards along them to gain access to borders for weeding, leaf clearing, gentle forking over and planting.

3 Birds are more obvious in the garden in winter when busy foraging for food, seeds, fruits, insects and slugs. Feeders filled with quality wild bird food and a constant supply of water will help see them through winter.

4 Avoid treading all over the garden when the ground is wet. Keep off frozen lawns – otherwise grass will be damaged.

Acanthus mollis has one of the most structural and loveliest seedheads. Allow the seeds to fall naturally and in warm areas new plants will germinate in a non-invasive way.

planting projects

tulips for a spring border 80

wild planting under trees 82

simple backdrop for climbers 84

lightening a dull corner 86

delicate blooms for late spring 88

focus on ferns 90

plants for a wildlife pond 92

heady scents for evening *94*

colourful carpeting plants 96

cool blue miniature pool 98

blazing annuals for high summer 100

no-fuss vegetables 102

bold foliage 104

instant structure and height 106

eye-catching container 108

aromatic mixed lavender border 110

quick evergreen screen 112

willow-weave herb basket 114

tropical flamboyance 116

long-season ornamental planting 118

sunny group for a winter porch 120

tulips for a spring border

As long as there is space to dig a narrow hole between existing plants, bulbs like tulips and narcissi can be added without the need to clear wide patches of ground. This works beautifully, because in spring the narrow stems rise above emerging perennials and the bulb leaves can die back naturally while being masked by the foliage of their companions. In a border like this, where there are generous clumps of fresh green and white Solomon's seal (*Polygonatum* x *hybridum*) and euphorbias flowering in shades of acid-yellow and purple-red, the tulips work best in small groups dotted about. Rather than sprinkling different-coloured tulips throughout, exercise restraint and use one variety, chosen to complement the colours of established plants. This has a stronger, unifying effect.

Tulips rarely give as good a performance in successive years and bulbs are often moved around by digging and weeding. I prefer to lift tulips so that a completely new colour scheme can be tried out without last year's flowers popping up to ruin the display. The best time to plant tulips is late autumn. Narcissi and crocus should be planted during early and mid-autumn (see pages 26–7).

Before you begin

Tidy a section of border by pulling out weeds and moving or adding any herbaceous perennials. If the border has no spring perennials, it might be nice to add some like these, or yellow-flowered leopard's bane (*Doronicum*) or summer snowflake (*Leucojum aestivum*).

Vibrant groups of 'High Society' tulips glow against *Euphorbia polychroma* (foreground right) and graceful sprays of Solomon's seal (*Polygonatum*) with its tiny white bells. Later, these will melt into the background as summer-flowering plants push through.

What you need
• narrow border fork, trowel

New plants
Tulip bulbs x 20
('High Society', shown here, is a Triumph tulip type, single, with brilliant red petals edged with orange. It flowers in mid- to late spring, H35–60cm/14–24in).

Half-hour planting
1 Find a suitable-sized gap, then fork over the soil gently to loosen it.
2 Set the bulbs out on the soil in groups of five, roughly 13cm/5in apart.
3 Using the trowel, dig a hole to plant each bulb about 13cm/5in deep.

Aftercare

• When the bulbs have finished flowering, deadhead by cutting off the old flower and its stalk. Some gardeners remove just the developing seed capsule, but I think the naked stalk looks rather silly.

• Allow the foliage to die back naturally, so that the bulb has at least six weeks to refuel itself for the following year, then dig up the bulbs carefully.

• Dry the bulbs off by spreading them out on racks in a dry place, preferably in the sun – they can be planted out elsewhere in late autumn.

• One of the best ways of using a mixture of second-year tulips is to plant them out into a cutting garden of flowers for the house. Any spare corner of soil will do but it should be in sun, and for best results well-dug and conditioned.

wild planting under trees

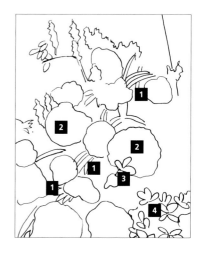

IN THIS CITY GARDEN, A MIXED PLANTING of euonymus, euphorbia, bluebells and lamium introduces a fresh, country note under the still leafless trees in spring. Spanish bluebells (*Hyacinthoides hispanica*) are prolific spreaders so you may be welcome to take some from a friend's garden. Daintier common bluebells (*H. non-scripta*) would do just as well, but never take them from the wild. Plant dormant bulbs in autumn, or move plants 'in the green' in spring. Dig carefully, as they are deep-rooted. *Lamium galeobdolon* is a common evergreen perennial in many gardens, so a friend may be able to offer you some – in which case, go for four or five roots. Alternatively, try variegated *L. g.* 'Hermann's Pride' or *L. orvala* with plain leaves and purple flowers. They are not invasive but are harder to track down. The delicate-looking but robust foam flower (*Tiarella wherryi* is my favourite) would do well in this position.

New plants
1 *Hyacinthoides hispanica* x 20
2 *Euphorbia amygdaloides* var. *robbiae* (Mrs Robb's bonnet) x 3
3 *Lamium galeobdolon* (yellow archangel) x 1
4 *Euonymus fortunei* 'Emerald 'n' Gold' x 1

Before you begin
Neaten any turf edge and, using a fork, loosen as much soil as possible without disturbing too many roots, but remove any weeds.

What you need
- wheelbarrow, hoe, bucket, spade, trowel
- soil conditioner
- gloves

Half-hour planting
1 If the soil is dry, water well. Allow the water to soak in, then add plenty of soil conditioner.
2 Make sure the plants are moist at the roots. Dunk them in a bucket of water if necessary.
3 With luck, the pots of euphorbia will be generous enough to divide into three or four plants. Wearing gloves (the sap can be an irritant), carefully loosen the soil and divide, cutting through stems where necessary.
4 Set the plants out. Start with the euonymus, and scatter the others randomly around it, aiming for a natural look.
5 Plant everything, then water in thoroughly.

Aftercare
- Water the plants often during the first summer.
- Yellow archangel is potentially invasive. Pull out unwanted plants and move others around.
- Bluebell leaves must remain on the plants for six weeks after flowering to fuel the bulbs; remove when they turn yellow.

TIP Peg one or two lower stems of the euonymus into the ground, using a 'U' bend of wire. In a year's time, these 'layers' will have rooted and can be used to extend the planting.

Semi-wild plants work well under trees and shrubs. They are tolerant of dry shade, and need little maintenance. Just fine-tune the planting in spring and autumn.

ELDERLY OR DILAPIDATED FENCES are a tricky problem to solve quickly and cheaply. Replacing them can be disruptive to the garden and also to neighbourly relations, if the responsibility rightfully rests next door. Painting is an option, but the fence needs to be in good condition and whacky colours can turn out to be big mistakes. This light bamboo screening is an ideal solution as it can be tacked on easily with a staple gun. It will last for several years, it can be covered with climbers and it is easy to replace when it becomes too weathered. To cover the fence and enjoy these ipomoeas in one season, tackle this project in spring.

Before you begin

Detach and lay down any existing climbing plants (they may need light pruning). To make a smooth base for the screen, brush down and patch up the fence, hammering any wonky panels to the posts. If the bamboo screen needs trimming, measure it first, then lay it down and cut it in a straight line with a pair of secateurs, chopping between the wires binding the stems together.

Although *Ipomoea tricolor* 'Heavenly Blue' is usually available in garden centres as plants during late spring, it is more easily obtainable by seed. It germinates well indoors, but early sowings are a mistake, as plants tend to flounder, turning white in the low light and cool temperatures of early spring. A mid- to late spring sowing will see seedlings romp away in a greenhouse or on the windowsill.

What you need
• roll of bamboo screening (wide enough to fit height of fence)
• staple gun, ball of string, knife
• trowel, fork
• soil conditioner, slow-release fertilizer

New plants
Ipomoea tricolor 'Heavenly Blue' (morning glory) x 8

Half-hour fixing and planting

1 Ask someone to hold the bamboo screen in place while you staple it to the fence.
2 Lightly fork soil conditioner and slow-release fertilizer over the border.
3 Use the trowel to dig a hole for the first plant, 15cm/6in from the base of the fence/screen. Lay a curl of string in the hole, then place the roots of the first plant on top. Fill and firm in.
4 Wind the string around the stem of the plant, then take it up and secure it to the top of the fence or screen with string.
5 Repeat for the other plants, setting them in a line about 23cm/9in apart, and water them all in thoroughly.

Aftercare
• Guard against slugs and snails while the plants become established (see page 168).
• Water if the soil becomes dry, but once established ipomoeas are reliably drought-tolerant.
• Applying liquid fertilizer every two weeks will ensure better growth and more flowers.
• When cold autumn weather ends the display, pull the plants up and replace with permanent climbers such as jasmine, clematis or Chilean potato vine. You can still add ipomoeas to these in the following spring.

The soft colour of bamboo hides a multitude of sins and provides a lovely backdrop to these morning glory, *Ipomoea tricolor* 'Heavenly Blue'. They may resemble bindweed, but as annuals, they pose no threat to the garden.

planting projects

lightening a dull corner

THIS TREATMENT WILL FILL A SUNNY OR SEMI-SHADED SITE roughly 1.5m/5ft long and 1.2m/4ft wide. There are already a variety of surfacing materials here, including turf, paving and timber, so adding a simple water feature, a few plants and some pebbles to fill the gaps should draw everything together as well as reflect light. Partially filled water features are safer for children using the garden and make convenient birdbaths and drinking areas for wildlife.

A potted larch is making a useful backdrop here and certainly produces bright young foliage in spring. I would aim to replace this with a permanent evergreen to provide winter interest, perhaps a variegated pittosporum, or silvery elaeagnus (page 144).

You can tackle this project any time, but it is best done in spring. You might need two half-hours for it: one for placing the hard materials and one for the planting.

Before you begin

Clear the area before starting; straighten the turf edge, fork over and weed the soil in the bed. In the meantime think about a good position for the bowl of water.

What you need

- wheelbarrow, bucket
- fork, spade, trowel
- watering can
- spirit level
- soil conditioner

Hard materials

- watertight glazed pot, at least 45cm/18in diameter
- large stones, 20–23cm/8–9in long x 7
- medium stones, 13–15cm/ 5–6in long x 20
- bagful of shingle or pebbles, roughly 5cm/2in diameter

New plants

See opposite.

Half-hour planting

1 Dig a shallow hole to take the base of the bowl, and position it with a good depth of rim sitting above the soil as in the picture. Place the spirit level across the top to make sure it is level. Firm the soil around it with your hands.

2 Arrange the large stones around the pot, reserving some to go inside.

3 Make sure that the plants are moist, then arrange them around the stones and slabs.

4 Using the spade for large plants and trowel for smaller ones, plant them, adding generous quantities of soil conditioner to the soil as you plant.

5 Finish off by arranging the medium and small-sized stones and pebbles around the plants.

6 Place the stones in the water feature and fill.

Aftercare

- All the new plants are drought- tolerant, but water through the first summer if necessary.
- Prune the sage hard in spring to encourage compact growth – light cropping for the kitchen benefits the plant, which becomes bushier as a result.

TIP Avoid using tiny stones such as pea shingle in gardens, because they have a habit of sticking to feet and trailing over lawns and into the house.

planting projects

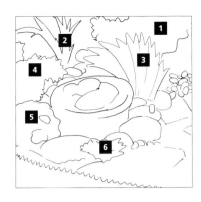

New plants

1 *Sedum spectabile* 'Brilliant Variegated' (ice plant) x 1 (or use *S. alboroseum* 'Mediovariegatum')

2 *Iris pallida* 'Variegata' x 1

3 *Juncus effusus* (soft rush) x 1

4 *Salvia officinalis* 'Icterina' (sage) x 3

5 *Euphorbia dulcis* 'Chameleon' x 1

6 *Ajuga reptans* cv. (bugle) x 2

This project makes good use of plants with light, bright foliage and light-reflecting stone mulches. Even whiter stones could also be used, or perhaps seaside shells. Instead of a water feature, one large major stone could be used. Choose carefully from a good builder or stone merchant, concentrating on a low, smooth shape and pale colour.

delicate blooms for late spring

SOME OF THE CLASSIEST FLOWERS of late spring and early summer can be easily added to any border to create loose drifts, and self-seeding or spreading plants are especially useful. Bearded iris, aquilegias and sweet rocket are three stalwarts at their best from spring to summer, before most of the roses appear.

Blue or mauve tones from a huge choice of bearded iris cultivars work best with deep purple and red aquilegias, but there are other blending colour variations for both types of plant. Aquilegias reach a height of 75cm/30in, sweet rocket 90cm/36in. Dwarf iris start from 45cm/18in in height and flower from mid-spring. Taller iris types are 70cm/28in high and more, and flower into early summer.

Early autumn is the best time to plant sweet rocket and bearded iris, though aquilegias can be added any time. Aquilegias can also be raised from seed. Plan ahead and sow during the preceding spring, following the method described on pages 24–5; the plants will be ready to transplant during autumn. If you plant in autumn, the roots will colonize the soil during winter. All plants should flower the following year.

Before you begin

Find a sunny strip of border measuring roughly 1.5m/5ft wide by at least 90cm/3ft deep, where a sprinkling of existing perennials will come through to flower during mid- and late summer. As you remove weeds and dead stems, identify gaps and fork soil conditioner into the topsoil.

Billowing tall blue iris, purple and mauve aquilegias and pale, fragrant sweet rocket bridge the gap between spring and midsummer. Use these between plants in a narrow border, or enjoy them as underplantings for a backdrop of climbing or rambling roses. After flowering, a border sort-out (see pages 48–9) will clear the way for later-flowering perennials thrusting their way forward.

What you need
• fork, spade, trowel

New plants
bearded iris x 2
Aquilegia vulgaris (columbine) x 8
Hesperis matronalis (sweet rocket) x 5

Method
1 If using potted plants, set them out on the ground in the gaps in the border.
2 Plant the iris first. Use the spade to take out a hole large enough to take the roots, then make a little centre mound for the rhizome to sit on. The top of the rhizome can then rest at the surface, while the roots are nicely spread out and down into the hole. Cover the roots with soil, firm in and water.
3 Plant the other two types of plant. If both are being lifted and transplanted, plant a couple of plants at a time to prevent the roots of the others from drying out.

Aftercare
• Aquilegias and sweet rocket are great self-seeders, so encourage this by allowing the seed heads to develop. Of the seeds that germinate, many will die off when shaded out by surrounding plants. Collect and keep some seed (see pages 70–1) for future sowings.
• Although sweet rocket may last another year, I find it best to pull this out and start again.
• Make sure the iris is not swamped by other plants, because its rhizomes like to feel the sun in order to flower well the following year.

UNTIDY AREAS BEHIND SHEDS OR AMONG TREES, and dark corners shaded by walls, are ideal for Victorian-style fern gardens. Most ferns appreciate dappled shade and moist soil. For drier areas, choose the beautiful shield fern (*Polystichum setiferum*) and its cultivars. There are many hardy ferns available, but stick to two or three types for a more natural effect. If there are no trees as such, introduce a few logs to create a woodland feel and encourage insects (which in turn provide food for birds), and moss will grow on the logs. Ferneries succeed best when the planting is kept simple, but add some bluebells and primroses (*P. vulgaris*) for spring, martagon lilies for summer and bugbane (*Cimicifuga racemosa*) for later. Planting ferns is best done between early autumn and spring.

LEFT Ideal for smaller places in gardens are the shining, decorative fronds of Japanese painted fern (*Athyrium niponicum* var. *pictum*). Here at the back are long, narrow fronds of Mrs Frizell's lady fern (*Athyrium filix-femina* 'Frizalliae'), and at the front are the divided fronds of *Adiantum pedatum*. With them are a scattering of white starry flowers of woodruff (*Galium odoratum*) and, top left, the silver-spotted foliage of *Pulmonaria saccharata* 'Leopard'.

OPPOSITE In a wooded garden area, a good, strong clump of hart's tongue in the foreground shines luxuriantly in front of a leaning trunk, and contrasts with the more feathery, wilder-looking male ferns behind.

Before you begin

Dig out weeds such as brambles, nettles, ground elder and bindweed, and move any debris off informal pathways.

What you need

- fork, spade, trowel
- soil conditioner
- watering can

New plants

Dryopteris felix-mas (male fern) x 3
Asplenium scolopendrium (hart's tongue fern) x 2

Half-hour planting

1 Decide where the ferns are to go and fork the ground over, targeting an area at least ten times larger than the ferns' roots. Remove weeds, old roots and other debris.
2 Spread soil conditioner over the turned soil and fork in.
3 Plant the ferns, using a trowel for small-sized ferns and the spade to make holes for the larger ones.
4 Water in well.

Aftercare

- Root out any troublesome weeds as they appear.

plants for a wildlife pond

GARDEN PONDS ARE AN ENDLESS SOURCE OF FASCINATION. Apart from providing a different growing environment, the pond is home to aquatic and amphibious creatures, and is also an important source of drinking water for animals, birds, butterflies and bees.

Ordinary ponds without a good balance of plantlife often turn green and soupy when algal growth suddenly accelerates with the increased warmth and light of summer. Aquatic plants compete successfully with the algae by taking up nutrients with their roots and shading the water with their leaves, robbing the algae of food, light and warmth. Submerged or oxygenating aquatics like hornwort (*Ceratophyllum demersum*) and pondweed (*Lagarosiphon major*) live mainly below the surface, water lilies and water hawthorn root underwater but bear floating leaves, the whole plants of water soldier and water hyacinth including their roots float or hang in the water and marginals, for instance the spectacular *Iris ensata* hybrids and marsh marigolds, stand half in, half out but also cast shade.

Adding a marginal or any aquatic plant can be done throughout the year, but spring is the best season. Aim to shade about half of the pond surface with foliage.

Before you begin

Check the water depth where the new plant is to sit (generally the label indicates depth required above the pot). Remove dead leaves and excess weed growth to make space. Repotting new aquatic plants is not strictly necessary, but some need it to grow well.

A water plantain is selected for planting from a tempting group of marginal aquatics including water iris, marsh marigold, bogbean (*Menyanthes trifoliata*) and skunk cabbage.

What you need
- aquatic baskets (a little larger than the plant containers)
- some hessian
- good loam or aquatic compost
- knife, shingle for the top, bricks

New plant
Alisma plantago-aquatica (water plantain) x 1

Half-hour planting
1 Place a hessian liner inside a basket and put some compost or soil in the base.
2 Remove the water plantain from its pot, cutting the plastic to save any roots that have grown through the holes.
3 Fill soil around the plant, topping off with shingle (**A**).
4 Add bricks if necessary to raise the plant to the correct height (the water plantain's pot should be 5–25cm/2–10in below the surface); lower the plant into the water (**B**).

Aftercare
- Stop other established spreading plants from encroaching the new plant.

A

Tips on pond plants

• Repot aquatics in shade, as hot sun might scorch previously submerged leaves.

• Choose plants in keeping with the pond. This water plantain, a native plant which seeds itself, was added to a natural-looking wildlife pond where plants are allowed to spread at random.

• Oxygenating weed, bought in bunches with metal weights attached, can be thrown into ponds with soil at the bottom. For a new, empty pond, pot the ends of the bunches first.

Even in early summer and in full sun, this pond water is as clear as crystal, largely because of its marvellous population of aquatic plants. Aquatic plants grow fast, which is a boon for new ponds, but means they have to be thinned constantly to stop them from occupying all the water space.

B

heady scents for evening

THERE ARE SO MANY GOOD PLANTS AND IDEAS current in gardening that it helps to focus on what a family needs. Here, a small courtyard garden is looking smart and well-furnished for a family who enjoy sitting out on summer evenings, relaxing with friends after busy lives at work during the day. A 'quick' screen of bamboo canes stapled to an old fence (see pages 84–5) creates a light backdrop for (from left to right) pittosporum, lesser catmint (*Calamintha nepeta* 'White Cloud'), golden hop, hydrangea and bamboo. Additions of fragrant, pale-flowered plants like lilies, petunias and honeysuckles glisten in the twilight or glow in the light of a few candles.

Planting up pots of lilies for a patio should be done in early spring, when there will be plenty of lily bulbs for sale. Alternatives to the lilies suggested here include *Lilium regale*, a reliable pale-flowered lily that comes into bloom just before 'Casa Blanca'. Pale pink, almost glistening 'Marco Polo' also gives excellent results.

Before you begin
Spend a half-hour tidying the existing backdrop. Remove dead leaves from plants and clip off any flower heads from last year. Sweep the patio on which the pots of lilies are to be placed.

What you need
- wheelbarrow or potting tidy (for mixing and containing compost)
- a bag each of John Innes no. 2 and soil-less potting compost
- large matching pots, at least 30cm/12in diameter x 5
- crocks or broken polystyrene
- watering can

New plants
Lilium 'Casa Blanca' bulbs x 3
Lilium longiflorum bulbs x 3
White petunias (e.g. large-flowered Grandiflora Group) x 5

Half-hour planting
1 Mix the composts together in equal quantity, using the wheelbarrow or potting tidy.
2 Put crocks over the bases of the pots, then some compost.
3 Arrange three lily bulbs per large pot, so that when covered, they will be 8–10cm/3–4in or so deep. Cover with compost, label and stand the pots in position before watering in thoroughly (this way there is less weight to carry). Alternatively, grow the bulbs on in a separate standing area until buds form.
4 Plant five petunias in each of the three remaining pots and water in well.

Aftercare
- Water the pots regularly. Feed weekly with a well-balanced liquid formula when the stems are established and growing.

planting projects

• Push a few twiggy sticks in around the lilies to support their growing stems, especially if it is at all windy.

• After flowering, allow the lilies to die back naturally; continue to water them when dry. They can either be planted out in autumn, or encouraged to grow again in their pots.

ABOVE A massed display of lily and petunia blooms coincides with those balmy summer evenings when the family want to sit outdoors.

LEFT Glistening at twilight, pure white flowers, like this heavily fragrant tobacco plant, *Nicotiana alata*, have the power to glow in the dark. Modern, day-performing types have little scent.

THE ULTIMATE LOW-MAINTENANCE SOLUTION is ground cover, which smothers the soil, making a strong network of roots underground and knitting together over the soil's surface. Weeds cannot germinate or set root and the soil is shaded from the drying effects of sun and wind, which benefits the plants. Ground-cover plants are good for wildlife, which flourishes under the moist leafy canopy.

The simplest and most effective use of ground cover is to use one sort of plant as a carpet. Here, a mass of ice plant (*Sedum*) fills the gap between the sweeping stems of *Viburnum plicatum* and the lawn edge. The colours blend beautifully in autumn, when the viburnum leaves flush with pink before falling, just as the sedums come into bloom. These are deciduous and will die back for winter. Evergreen alternatives include bugle, ivies and epimedium.

This is an ideal treatment for a sunny area roughly 90cm/3ft square. The optimum planting times are autumn or spring.

Before you begin

Trim the lawn edge, remove weeds and if the soil is dense and clay-like, fork in a 50:50 mix of soil conditioner and sharp grit. Eight sedums will give quick cover. If you can't beg some from a friend's garden and have to buy plants, three large potfuls may be sufficient as they are easy to divide.

This bugle (*Ajuga reptans* 'Atropurpurea') makes a superb carpet of neat purple-bronze leaves, joined in late spring by candles of blue flowers. There are several other good cultivars including dark *A. r.* 'Braunherz' and *A. r.* 'Multicolor'. Under ideal conditions, where soil is moist and partially shaded, one small plant is capable of spreading 90cm/3ft in a single season.

What you need
- spade, trowel
- watering can

New plants
Sedum 'Ruby Glow' (ice plant) x 8 (*S. spectabile* is a good alternative – see page 141).

Half-hour planting

1 Set the plants out over the area to be covered, spacing them about 30cm/12in apart.
2 Dig holes with a trowel for small plants, but use a spade for larger roots, and plant, firming them in carefully.
3 Water the plants in well.

Aftercare

• Weed between the sedums as they settle down.
• The dying flower heads are attractive, especially when rimed with frost, so leave them on until they turn black and soggy.
• Lift, divide and replant every three years (see pages 34–5);

Carpeting plants are great for hiding patches of bare earth under shrubs. Even when dormant, their root mass discourages weeds.

otherwise clumps become too large and die off in the middle.
• Avoid over-feeding sedums, or they become too large and leafy.

cool blue miniature pool

EVEN THE MINUTEST AREA OF WATER brings a touch of magic to a garden, offering reflections and a place for bees and birds to drink. This blue-glazed basin has been chosen to complement the plants, but any material will do as long as it is frost-proof.

The grasses, bamboos and hostas I have suggested here are all easy to source and suit either sun or light shade. The benefits of plants in pots are that they can be moved around easily, slug control is easier for hostas raised above the soil and bamboos are not tempted to spread. But if watering is too onerous, they can be planted out.

Before you begin

Prepare an area of small-grade stone chippings about 1.8m/6ft wide and 1.2m/4ft deep. Stone chippings bed down better and tend to move about less than shingle. If the area contains weeds, tread over the soil and rake to obtain a smooth level. To avoid future weeding, consider laying a polypropylene membrane to suppress germination of seeds or regrowth of perennial weeds. Spread a generous layer of stones on top. If the plants are to remain in pots, perhaps spend another half an hour repotting them into attractive containers.

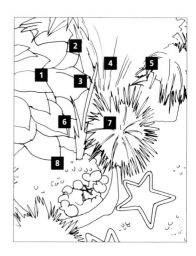

New plants

1 *Hosta* cv. x 1
2 *Bashania fargesii* (bamboo) x 1
3 *Milium effusum* 'Aureum' (Bowles' golden grass) x 1
4 *Stipa tenuissima* (feather grass) x 1
5 *Carex* sp. x 1
6 *Iris laevigata* 'Variegata' x 1
7 *Festuca glauca* 'Blaufuchs' (blue fescue) x 2
8 *Nymphaea* 'Pygmaea Helvola' (pygmy water lily) x 1

What you need

- waterproof bowl, 60cm/2ft wide and at least 38cm/15in deep
- bucket or can of water
- trowel
- stone chippings

Half-hour planting

1 Position the bowl and set it into the stones so that the top is completely level.

2 Place the plants, apart from the water lily and the water iris, around the bowl, not quite touching, so that air can circulate.

3 If planting any of the plants out, remove the bowl. Scrape the gravel away from the soil with the trowel (if you laid a membrane, make a cross-cut in it), and plant. Replace the gravel. Remove any excess soil.

4 Fill the bowl with water almost to the top. Spread a layer of gravel over the soil of the water-lily pot and gently tilt the pot into the water.

5 Repeat with the water iris, placing it towards the edge.

6 Top up the bowl with water, right up to the rim.

These plants are all trouble-free except for the hosta, which may become slug-ravished. If so, try instead ferns or a pot of *Alchemilla mollis* (see page 134). The decorative plants in the bowl serve to keep the water healthy; without them, algae would turn the water an unsightly green. Once the design is in place, be on the look-out for details like the stars and blue chippings to add extra sparkle.

planting projects

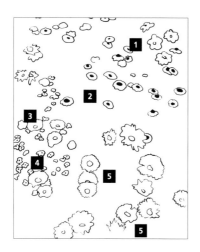

New plants

1 *Cosmos sulphureus* x 2

2 *Zinnia boliviensis* (or other tall single type) x 3

3 *Rudbeckia hirta* 'Marmalade' x 2

4 *Tagetes* (e.g. Gem Series) x 3

5 *Calendula officinalis* x 3

What you need

• trowel, watering can

• soil conditioner, fertilizer (e.g. pelleted chicken manure)

Half-hour planting

1 Set the plants out in a random but pleasing way, roughly 23cm/9in apart.

2 Plant, using the trowel, starting at the back of the area and working forwards.

3 Water in thoroughly.

Aftercare

• Guard against slugs and snails, especially during the few days following planting.

• Weed between the plants as and when they establish.

• Water only when a long drought ensues, then apply copious quantities of water to the roots in one go.

• Deadheading will encourage the flowering to continue well into autumn.

ANNUALS AND TENDER PERENNIALS CAN BE DESCRIBED as high-maintenance plants, because they need replacing every year. Yet they deserve a place in every garden, where a late spring planting, after all danger of frost has passed, will supply a quick fix of summer colour. Annuals are ideal for filling gaps in new gardens before more permanent plants knit together, but more than this, they allow the summer and winter display to vary from year to year.

A good place to grow annuals and exciting but transitory and high-maintenance plants such as dahlias, canna and even pumpkins is what I call a 'bit border'. This is the fun border every gardener needs where anything goes and everything changes each year. Grow tall tithonias one year, low mesembryanthemums the next, and just experiment. Use it for seedbeds and tulips for cut flowers too.

Annuals are at their most stunning when used informally, as with this mass of daisy-like flowers. For a similar effect, choose plants which have a tall, natural look with many flower stems terminating in single blooms. Plant in late spring or early summer in full sun. This planting will fill a space 90cm/3ft wide and 1.2m/4ft deep.

Before you begin

Fork over a patch of soil to remove weeds. If the soil is in good heart, spread soil conditioner and fertilizer over the surface and fork in. Where it is solid and uncultivated, proper digging a few weeks beforehand will work wonders (see page 22).

This massed informal planting of different golden daisy-like flowers is inspired. It avoids the compact types bred for conventional bedding out, with the exception of the tagetes, whose dainty orange flowers are an understorey to the taller daisies. When buying the plants, it is a good idea to choose them already in bloom to be sure of obtaining the desired range and blend of colours.

planting projects

SPACE CAN ALWAYS BE FOUND for growing plants to eat, either in beds or tucked into gaps between ornamental plants. Herbs and salad plants partly concealed by flowers often avoid the attention of pests. Courgettes, French beans, red-leaved lettuce (slugs tend to disregard these), bush tomatoes and blocks of sweetcorn are all suitable. Crop rotation – changing where a crop grows from year to year – is good practice as it helps prevent disease. To plant these courgettes, you just need to allocate half an hour in late spring or early summer.

Before you begin

Well-cultivated soil is essential for healthy crops. Where ground is hard and compacted, digging and incorporating soil conditioner (see page 22) is the best treatment. From then on, as long as you avoid trampling, an annual application of soil conditioner should prove adequate. A general-purpose fertilizer will help on poor soils.

Bright courgette flowers and young sweetcorn (right) contrast with purple lavender. Interplanted with the sweetcorn are lettuces under plastic-bottle cloches, which keep heat and moisture in and slugs out. Planting sweetcorn in blocks helps windborne pollen circulate more effectively for the pollination necessary to produce corn on the cob. Smaller groups can be used to add height to ordinary borders. Plant out seedlings when danger of frost has passed, 38cm/15in apart, setting each in a shallow 'dish' so that water channels to the roots.

What you need

- fork, trowel
- watering can
- buckets of well-rotted garden compost or horse manure x 3 (or best soil conditioner)
- courgette plants x 3
- straw

Half-hour planting

1 Allow for plants to be spaced 75cm/30in apart, decide where they will grow and empty a bucketful of compost on each site. Fork this in lightly, leaving a low mound. Make a slight dish in the top of each mound.
2 Use the trowel to plant one courgette into each dish. Water in and mulch with straw.

Aftercare

• Courgettes are thirsty plants and will benefit from regular watering during droughts.
• Slugs and snails make a feast of young courgette seedlings, so use your preferred method of control (see pages 168–9) and inspect at night by torchlight to make sure it is working. As they mature, the plants will be less vulnerable, though slugs may eat developing courgettes.
• When the flowers start to open, feed weekly with a tomato-type fertilizer.
• Fortnightly foliar feeds with liquid seaweed will work wonders, too.
• Cut the courgettes off with a knife; twisting off may damage the plant's growing stem.
• Crop regularly to encourage more flowers and prevent courgettes from growing into marrows.

TIP Courgettes are easy to grow from seed. Place three seeds into each shallow 'dish', and push lightly into the soil, covering by no more than their own depth. Water and mulch as for plants, but then thin out the two weaker seedlings, to leave one to develop. If all seedlings in one mound fail, transplant a spare from another while it is still small, preferably at the two-leaf stage.

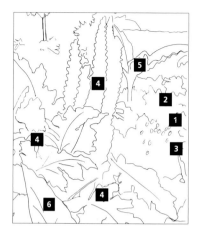

THE PRESENCE OF PLANTS WITH BOLD FOLIAGE adds a fun, sculptural element to a garden. Structure is important to design and achieving it with plants is a useful alternative to costly or time-consuming hard landscaping. The project here is to add a colony of easy-to-grow, hardy evergreen bear's breeches (*Acanthus mollis*) to an existing border. These remain architectural throughout winter, when their summer flowers turn to stately seed heads. The effect is further enhanced by exotic-looking banana and giant taro and fatsia-like leaves of rice-paper plant, though in some areas these cannot be left to grow outside permanently.

Existing plants

1 *Zantedeschia* (arum lily)

2 *Tetrapanax papyrifer* (rice-paper plant)

3 *Darmera peltata*

New plants

4 *Acanthus mollis* (bear's breeches) x 3

Added 'indoor' plants

5 *Musa basjoo* (banana)

6 *Alocasia* (giant taro)

Acanthus is a show-stopper when its primeval-looking foliage is joined by tall spires of purple and white flowers. Rice-paper plant and 'hardy' banana will only withstand a modicum of frost and may require protection during winter. The giant taro, *Alocasia*, will certainly need a warm greenhouse to see it through cold winters.

Before you begin

Select an area which can accommodate a clump of acanthus, then make space about 90cm/3ft square. Ensure the soil is weeded and well conditioned.

What you need

- spade or trowel
- watering can

Half-hour planting

1 Set the new plants out on the soil in triangular formation, about 75cm/30in apart, and then stand back to check their position, trying to imagine their size in a couple of seasons.

2 If the plants are large with bare roots (as may be the case, perhaps, if you have 'purloined' them from a neighbouring garden), dig a hole with the spade and firm them in well. Use the trowel if they are in small pots. Either way, within a year each plant should expand to at least 60cm/24in in good soil.

3 Water the plants in well.

Aftercare

- Keep surrounding soil weed-free until the acanthus plants are well established.
- Water during dry spells until the root system is self-sufficient; thereafter, acanthus will prove reliably drought-tolerant.
- No staking needed.

TIP Displaying suitable tropical plants or houseplants outdoors in summer is a good way of harnessing their exotic foliage at the same time as letting them enjoy better light and humidity.

planting projects

Although it is satisfying to replant a border, it is frustrating when the finished effort consists of small plants in a sea of dark soil. The beautiful garden-to-be has to live in the imagination until it has had time to mature. While you are waiting for plants to grow, instant height from an obelisk, a wigwam of poles or an arch supporting climbers such as the clematis pictured here can usefully punctuate the garden. For a quick, colourful, fragrant show a spring planting of sweet peas is hard to beat, while a climbing rose with a clematis growing through it doubles up on colour and interest.

A most effective quick fix for height is a metal or wooden obelisk, bought from garden centres or shows, or by mail order. The cheaper option, a wigwam of poles, relies on a source of rustic stems. Five or six straightish poles, from coppiced or pollarded hazel, about 2.2–2.5m/7–8ft high and 4cm/1.5in diameter, stuck firmly into the soil with their tops wired together, are ideal. It is almost worth planting hazel or willow in order to grow a supply of twigs and poles for garden work. They make a satisfyingly sustainable source – and they are much more attractive than rigid bamboo canes.

Before you begin

Ask someone to hold the obelisk or wigwam in place and view its effect from all angles before committing yourself to its position. Then, clear an area roomy enough to take the structure, moving any plants out of the way. Fork over the area , remove weeds and dig in soil conditioner.

What you need
- **metal or wooden obelisk**
- **fork, spade**
- **soil conditioner**
- **watering can**

New plant
Clematis 'Jackmanii Rubra' x 1
   (alternatives: *C.* 'Hagley Hybrid'
   or *C.* 'Ascotiensis')

Half-hour planting

1 Fix the obelisk in the ground (usually by driving its pointed metal feet into the soil).

2 Set the clematis to one side of the obelisk and plant, using the spade. Bury the stem of the clematis about 15cm/6in deeper than it was in the pot. This is to encourage new shoots to grow, should it suffer from wilt.

3 Mulch over the roots with soil conditioner, keeping it clear of the stem or stems.

Aftercare
- Prune this clematis to about 30cm/12in in early spring; this helps it branch and send up lots of healthy stems.
- For cultivars that start their flowering in early summer, do not prune hard thereafter but tidy by cutting back to the topmost pair of fat buds each year in early spring.
- Clematis respond well to a slow-release rose-type fertilizer applied once in spring, then mulched over the top.
- Alternatively, apply several liquid feeds up to midsummer.
- Water during droughts.

Clematis cling by means of leaf-stalk tendrils which wind themselves around the support structure and their own stems. Simply plant near the support, lean growths in the right direction and nature will usually do the rest. Clematis and climbing roses are made for each other (try *Rosa* 'Pink Bells', trained as a climber and teamed with dark maroon-red *Clematis* 'Niobe'). Clematis roots should be shaded from hot sun, so ensure that the leaves of herbaceous plants near by will protect them.

planting projects

eye-catching container

CONTAINERS FULL OF FLOWERS are a transitory and moveable feast in the garden, offering colour where needed as well as being neat. However, they must rely on a regular watering regime (or an automatic watering system), so do think about the implications of planting up too many. This one is designed to brighten a sunny position in the garden from early summer to autumn.

Planting a container will only be speedy if all the ingredients are assembled first. When shopping, be armed with a mental image of the pot and site (surrounding colours, whether sunny or shady). Rather than sticking to a list, choose the best plants available, looking for the main ones first (in this case the lantana). Select the rest to complement these. One or two colours are usually more effective than a riot.

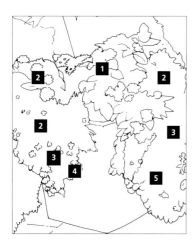

New plants
1 *Argyranthemum* cv. x 2
2 *Lantana camara* cv. x 2
3 White-flowered trailing lobelia x 8
4 *Helichrysum* x 4
5 White trailing million bells petunia x 1

Before you begin
If using an old pot, brush it out thoroughly. To prevent clay pots from sucking a lot of moisture from the compost, either pre-soak by sprinkling them with a watering can, then cover with an old wet towel, or line with black polythene punched with drainage holes at the base.

What you need
- large terracotta container, 38cm/15cm square at top
- crocks or broken polystyrene
- wheelbarrow or portable potting tray
- a bag each of John Innes potting compost no. 2 and soil-less potting compost
- slow-release fertilizer
- trowel
- watering can

Half-hour planting
1 Mix the two potting composts together in equal quantities, using the wheelbarrow or potting tray. Mix in some slow-release fertilizer.
2 Crock the pot base, covering the drainage hole with broken pot shards or polystyrene.
3 Add compost to reach the correct depth for the largest plant, firming gently as you go.
4 Place the argyranthemums in the middle, teasing out their roots (**A**).
5 Position the lantanas, adding compost around them, to reach the depth of the smaller plants. Position these around the edge, then check all the plant heights.
6 Fill in with compost around all the plants (**B**), firming gently. The compost should be 2.5cm/1in below the rim to allow for watering and root expansion.
7 Water in thoroughly, using a can with a rose so that the compost is not disturbed.

Aftercare
- Check the container morning and night for watering, come rain or shine; containers in the rain shadow of walls or fences often need a good soak, even

planting projects

108

after a downpour.

• The plants will benefit from a dose of liquid fertilizer, despite the slow-release fertilizer.

• Remove dead flowers to improve appearance and encourage new ones.

Four weeks after planting, the plants have knitted together. They should continue to open their yellow and white blooms until autumn.

THERE IS NOTHING MORE SATISFYING TO THE EYE than a well-defined border edge. Once this is in place, the plantings inside automatically seem more contained and organized. Bricks make a strong, attractive edging, but they really need to be set into concrete to remain firm and not be dislodged by the roots of plants and weeds. Laying bricks may be beyond the scope of the time-pressed gardener, but a planted lavender edging is effective as well as quick and easy. About eight plants, enough to clothe an edge 2.5m/8ft long, can be planted out in half an hour, and the spaces between filled with thyme. Remember, bees love these plants, so avoid edging a narrow pathway with them, especially if anyone in the family reacts badly to bees or bee stings.

Think about whether to opt for a mix, or a more formal edge of identical plants. *Lavandula angustifolia* 'Munstead' is a popular choice for edgings because it is a compact 45cm/18in high. Because it is a selected clone, the plants will not vary in height or leaf colour, and will have the same shade of purple-blue flowers. To achieve a variety of height, leaf and flower colour as shown here, choose from any of the wide range of lavenders available. English lavender (*L.* x *intermedia* Old English Group) gives off the classic lavender perfume, while French lavender (*L. stoechas*), has a different, distinct aroma. Flower colours blend well together and include mauve, pink and white. Plants will take best if planted during autumn or spring.

Before you begin

Clear a space along the edge of the border, carefully moving plants out of the way. Fork the soil over and remove weeds. Condition sticky soil by adding sharp sand or coarse grit. Do not add a rich soil conditioner like well-rotted manure, because lavenders neither need nor like this.

What you need

- fork, spade, trowel
- sharp sand or coarse grit (if soil is sticky)
- stiff hand brush
- watering can

New plants

Mixed lavenders x 8 (*Lavandula angustifolia*, e.g. 'Munstead', 'Loddon Blue', 'Loddon Anna' or 'Twickel Purple')
Thymus citriodorus (lemon thyme) x 5

Lavenders knit together to make a colourful, aromatic edging. Alternative edging plants to try are hyssop and cotton lavender (*Santolina chamae-cyparissus*), suitable as long as they are clipped every spring. Classic box makes a more formal, evergreen edging. *Sedum spectabile* creates lovely glaucous mounds (see page 141), but only during summer. For interplanting try self-seeding purple violas, tiny pinks (*Dianthus*) or snow-in-summer (*Cerastium tomentosum*).

Half-hour planting

1 Set the lavenders out about 30cm/12in inside the border edge, and check that their spacing is even, 30cm/12in apart.

2 Plant, using a trowel or spade according to root size.

3 Set out the thymes here and there between the lavenders at the front, then plant these too.

3 Brush any soil off the path or edge, and water the plants in thoroughly.

Aftercare

• To keep lavender compact and stop plants growing woody at the base, shear old flower stems off in spring, cutting back into the growth beneath.

EVERY GARDEN NEEDS ITS WORKING OR UTILITY CORNER where shed and compost heap are kept, and in most cases these are best screened from view. Yet it is a pity to hide these fixtures completely, especially if they are attractively made. A shed peeping through greenery can make an appealing picture. Add a meandering path leading to it, and you relieve the stubborn rectangular shape of many gardens.

Though it is tempting to use trellis or fencing as a screen, it is easier and cheaper to put in a couple of evergreen shrubs. It takes only two to four years for them to grow tall enough to take on a major screening role. You could also use them to create dividers for the garden, so that it is transformed into several sections or glades. While you wait for the young plants to grow, infill the spaces with a hazel pole obelisk or wigwam for climbing plants (see page 106).

Living bamboos, with their swaying stems and whispering leaves, make lovely screens and are best left to grow naturally – there is no need to thin or remove lower sideshoots. The two plants I have chosen here will grow in sun or semi-shade and when reasonably mature, about five years after planting, will occupy a site 5m/16ft long and 1.2–1.8m/4–6ft wide. Plant in autumn or between then and spring when the soil is neither frozen nor waterlogged.

Before you begin

Give the shed or other fixtures a coat of paint or wood stain. Research possible plants and decide where they should go. Prepare the planting area by weeding, digging over the soil and adding soil conditioner.

A screen of bamboo and elaeagnus is enhanced by props. Large pots and vases are decorative enough to be left empty. Instead of elaeagnus you could use another evergreen shrub. Pittosporums for milder regions, the unusual *Itea ilicifolia*, *Fatsia japonica* for shade and reliable *Viburnum tinus* are all suitable and can be enlivened by the addition of late-flowering clematis.

What you need
- fork, spade
- soil conditioner
- wheelbarrow of mulching material
- watering can

New plants
Elaeagnus x *ebbingei* 'Gilt Edge'
Phyllostachys sp. (bamboo)

Half-hour planting

1 Choose the best position for the plants for obscuring the shed, and try to envisage their eventual height and spread.
2 For each plant, dig a generous hole. Fork over the bottom, adding more soil conditioner if the soil seems poor.
3 Plant to the correct height and water in thoroughly, using a 10-litre/2-gallon can on each.
4 Cover the surface with an 8cm/3in layer of mulch.

Aftercare

• Once the bamboo is established, keep an eye on its spread and restrict it using a sharp spade (wayward stems are relatively easy to curtail when young, but mature roots and stems are difficult to dig out).
• Control the size and shape of the elaeagnus using secateurs and loppers. It needs no pruning as such, but in a small garden some guidance is required.
• If the elaeagnus sends up shoots of all-green leaves, prune these out or the 'reversion', as it is known, will take over the whole shrub.

planting projects

Aromatic and useful, a collection of culinary herbs sits well in a any container. This rustic basket acts like a miniature raised bed and has been made by twisting flexible hazel stems around supports. (The supports are secured in the ground and woven *in situ*, in much the same way you would a wattle fence.) Turf has been used to line the inside to stop soil from falling out. However, it would be far simpler to buy a basket from a garden centre or florists'. It may be more tightly woven and will probably be lined, yet can still look rustic. Plants are available to buy in small pots during spring and summer, and, with care, the arrangement will last for two to three years.

Before you begin

If the basket is unlined, cut polythene to fit, to hold compost, piercing the base for drainage. Raising the basket off the soil on low bricks or tiles will delay the rotting of the base, so have these ready. Choose where you want to position the basket and place *in situ* before you plant to avoid moving it when it is heavy with soil and plants.

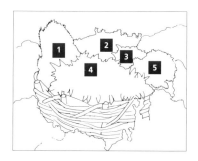

New plants in basket

1 *Foeniculum vulgare* (fennel) x 1

2 *Origanum vulgare* 'Gold Tip' (marjoram) x 1

3 *Salvia officinalis* 'Tricolor' (tricolor sage) x 1

4 *Salvia officinalis* 'Purpurascens' (purple sage) x 4

5 *Tanacetum parthenium* 'Aureum' (golden feverfew) x 1

What you need

- basket 60cm/24in diameter, plus polythene to line
- crocks, stones or polystyrene for drainage
- potting compost (a 50:50 mix of John Innes no. 2 and soil-less compost with added sharp sand or grit)
- fork, trowel, watering can
- 5 or 6 tiles or bricks to raise the basket off the soil

Half-hour planting

1 Place drainage material 5cm/ 2in over the lining and add a good layer of compost.

2 Shuffle herbs still in their pots around in the basket to get a satisfactory arrangement.

3 Remove the herbs from their pots, making sure they are placed at the correct height and about 15cm/6in apart. Fill in compost around their roots, firming gently. Leave a 2.5cm/ 1in margin of rim showing and tuck the liner out of sight.

4 Water in well to settle soil.

Aftercare

- Water when the surface of the compost dries out. Feed with a general-purpose liquid fertilizer about three times during the summer.
- If any dead flower stems look scruffy, cut them off but leave some seedheads to shelter insects for winter bird food.
- In spring, trim the sages to encourage a compact shape.

The prettiness of the herbs in the basket is accentuated by repeating or adding others such as thyme and borage around it. Buy about seven extra plants and arrange these outside the basket, about 30cm/12in apart.

planting projects

tropical flamboyance

THE AIM HERE IS TO IMPRESS. Without proper planning, gardens have a tendency to suffer from burn-out in late summer after the lush profusion earlier in the season. Fill this gap by adding carefully chosen plants in late spring or early summer, which will grow throughout the summer months to give a fiery performance when needed, and possibly on into autumn. These plants will cover an area roughly 1.2m/4ft square.

Before you begin

Weed the area carefully, loosening the soil with a fork, and add generous amounts of soil conditioner. Here there is a backdrop of vigorous pink-flowered Joe Pye weed (*Eupatorium purpureum*). A plant like this may need reducing to create space.

For an instant effect with the canna, buy a plant ready established in its pot. Cannas can be bought by mail order as small sections of rhizome, but these require skill and time to grow into plants large enough for a display in a single season.

What you need

- **wheelbarrow of soil conditioner**
- **bucket of water**
- **fork, spade**
- **watering can**

The fiery red of the dahlias and white spires of veronicastrum contrast well with the giant dark purple-green canna foliage. *Fatsia japonica*, aspidistra, phormium, *Melianthus major* and hardy Chusan palm (*Trachycarpus fortunei*) all contribute to a tropical effect. Use this small section of colour as an inspiration which can be added to every year to create a really hot border, but aim to limit the number of plants needing time-consuming overwintering.

New plants

Canna cv, e.g. 'Wyoming' (purple-leaved Indian shot) x 1

Veronicastrum virginicum f. *album* (white Culver's root) x 2

Crocosmia 'Lucifer' (montbretia) x 2

Dahlia 'Bishop of Llandaff' x 1

Half-hour planting

1 All plants must be moist at the roots, so dunk dry ones in a bucket of water to soak them thoroughly.

2 Position the new plants on the soil, trying to imagine their full size and juggling them about until you are satisfied.

3 Starting from the back, dig a generous hole for each plant, add more compost in the hole and to the replant soil, then settle them in firmly.

4 Water the plants in gently but thoroughly, using a can fitted with a rose, or a gentle spray with the hosepipe.

Aftercare

- Water the plants during dry periods.
- When you feel they have taken off, give liquid feeds with a general-purpose fertilizer fortnightly to stimulate growth.
- Most gardeners lift their cannas in autumn before the first frosts. Pot them up and keep in a frost-free shed or greenhouse, semi-dormant, until the following spring. In milder regions they can be left outside and will grow new shoots in spring.
- For dahlias it is much the same. In my Devon garden, I can risk leaving them out in well-drained soil. Where soil is cold and wet for long periods, lift the tubers after the first frosts, dry off and store half covered by dryish compost in a cool, frost-free place. Plant out the following spring.

planting projects

long-season ornamental planting

THIS PROJECT, OF DRIFTS OF LOW-MAINTENANCE PERENNIALS, was inspired by an experiment I tried in our last garden, as a domestic-scale version of the 'prairie plantings' of contemporary landscape designers, where natural-looking plants are carefully chosen to match prevailing soil and climate. Here biennials and perennials are introduced, then allowed to seed and spread. To follow spring bulbs are purple blooms of variegated honesty, bronze fennel, purple-leaved *Rosa glauca* and French lavender, with alliums and pink hybrid thrifts to see summer in. The added foxtail lilies and sea hollies will enhance high summer until the developing seedheads of autumn.

Planting of this kind suits a dry, poor, sandy soil and needs little attention other than pulling weeds and thinning unwanted honesty and fennel seedlings. This effect can be recreated in a sunny patch of ground 90cm/3ft wide by 1.2m/4ft deep. Plant in autumn or spring.

Before you begin
Weed the section of border carefully and remove dead bits and pieces. Avoid too much soil disturbance as there will be desirable seedlings coming through as well as weeds. Unless you have bare patches of soil, make spaces for the new plants. If buying the foxtail lilies as bulbs, examine them to make sure the roots are plump and healthy.

What you need
- spade
- buckets of soil conditioner x 2
- watering can

Existing plants
1 *Cupressus macrocarpa* 'Green Pillar'
2 *Chamaecyparis lawsoniana* 'Summer Snow'
3 *Nectaroscordum siculum*
4 *Foeniculum vulgare* 'Purpureum' (bronze fennel)
5 *Lavandula stoechas* 'Helmsdale'

6 *Lunaria annua* (honesty)
7 *Platycodon grandiflorus*
8 *Allium cristophii* (ornamental onion)

New plants
9 *Eremurus stenophyllus* (foxtail lily) x 2
10 *Eryngium bourgatii* (sea holly) x 1

Half-hour planting
1 Set the plants out on site, envisaging their ultimate size and imagining their blooms.

2 For each, dig a generous hole and mix soil conditioner in at the bottom and with the infill soil. The crowns of the foxtail lilies should ideally be covered by 15cm/6in of soil.
3 Water in well.

Aftercare
- Note where the foxtail lilies are to be sure not to disturb them while dormant in winter.
- Remove the fennel's dead flowerheads before seeds ripen, to avoid a forest of seedlings.

The bed in late summer, when the shimmering haze of fennel foliage and developing seedheads seems to match hot, dry days. Even during long rainless periods, these plants proved capable of holding their own without needing extra watering.

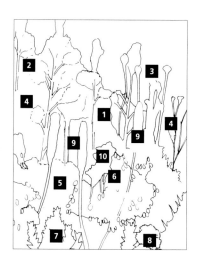

planting projects

MOST HOUSEHOLDS OFFER A RANGE of growing conditions for plants, both indoors and out, just waiting to be exploited. One such might be an unheated porch, a structure offering protection from frost, rain and cold winds, yet providing light and cool temperatures – particularly valuable for overwintering tender plants. Another use for it might be to give protection to hardy plants for winter and early spring displays which would be blown to smithereens out in the open.

Plant up this group during autumn, using good, but ordinary clay pots. Provide good-sized, glazed drip saucers to hold water.

Before you begin

Wash the glass of the porch down, inside and out, to let in maximum light. Clear and sweep the inside, ready to take the plants. If the pots have been used before, scrub them out.

What you need

- 6 clay pots: approx. 23cm/9in x 2 (1 full-sized, 1 shallow pan); 20cm/8in x 1; 15cm/6in x 1 and 13cm/5in x 2
- matching glazed saucers
- wheelbarrow or potting tidy of compost (50:50 John Innes no. 2 and soil-less potting compost)
- crocks, trowel
- moss for finishing off (buy small packets of sphagnum moss from florists or garden centres)
- watering can

New plants

Hebe pinguifolia 'Pagei' x 1
Hedera helix (variegated ivy)
Narcissus 'Tête-à-Tête' x 1 packet (about 10 bulbs)
Galanthus nivalis (snowdrops) x 1 packet bulbs (or 3 small potfuls; best bought 'in the green')
Iris danfordiae x 6 bulbs

Half-hour planting

1 Repot the hebe into the 20cm/8in pot and the ivy into a 15cm/6in pot.

2 Place some compost in the large 23cm/9in pot, then arrange the narcissus bulbs so that they are not quite touching and when covered will be buried by a good 8cm/3in of compost.

3 Plant the snowdrop bulbs in the shallower pot, or wait until spring to buy snowdrop plants, potting the three smaller containers into the large shallow pan.

4 Plant the iris bulbs, three per pot.

5 Water in all the plants and bulbs, using a rose on the can so as not to disturb the surfaces.

6 Top the pots with moss, to cover the bare soil. The hebe and ivy can go straight into the porch, but the bulbs can stand outside until they sprout.

Aftercare

- Outside, the bulbs should be covered by a 10cm/4in layer of old compost or sand, but in milder areas they will grow well with the pots uncovered, tucked out of the way.
- Ensure they do not dry out.
- After flowering, plant the bulbs straight into the garden where they can naturalize. The hebe and ivy will be better off outdoors in summer, so plant these out too, or repot the ivy.

An unheated, well-ventilated porch is an ideal showcase for hardy winter and spring plants, which provide a bright welcome for all who come to the door. Here is a selection of evergreens and bulbs in pots. From back to front: narcissi, an evergreen hebe, snowdrops (*Galanthus*), yellow iris and a variegated ivy (*Hedera helix*).

easy-care plants

bulbs and corms 124

annuals, biennials and tender perennials 127

vegetables and herbs 130

grasses and ferns 132

hardy perennials 134

shrubs 142

climbers and wall shrubs 150

trees 154

Y = RHS Award of Garden Merit

Allium cristophii Y
Ornamental onion

H 30–60cm/2–3ft S 18cm/7in

Bulbs are easy to plant between existing plants and leaves take up little space, in exchange for heads of purple-pink flowers up to 20cm/8in across. These fade to parchment and persist well into autumn. Team with yellow-flowered euphorbias, purple-leaved fennel and silvery lavenders.

POSITION In sun and well-drained soil. Plant 8cm/3in deep in autumn.

MAINTENANCE Seedheads are an attractive asset so leave to ripen. If undisturbed, the seeds scatter, allowing fine colonies to develop.

ALTERNATIVES Choose 90cm/3ft tall *A. hollandicum* 'Purple Sensation' for height. The swaying 75cm/30in stems of *A. sphaerocephalon* topped by small heads of dense, dark purple flowers are fun.

Allium cristophii

Crocus chrysanthus 'Snow Bunting'

Crocus chrysanthus 'Snow Bunting' Y

H and S 8cm/3in

Scatter these small and affordable crocus corms on borders or lawns, planting 8cm/3in deep where they fall. The smaller-flowered, early-flowering varieties are valuable for cheering up late winter and are most effective planted in drifts of single toning rather than mixed colours.

POSITION Plant in sun for flowers to open fully. Plants naturalize and increase in a well-drained soil.

MAINTENANCE Allow leaves to remain so that they die naturally.

ALTERNATIVES *C. c.* 'Prins Claus' is white inside with three mauve-blue blotches outside; 'Prinses Beatrix' is soft mauve-blue with a yellow centre and yellow-blooming 'Zwanenburg Bronze' Y is striped with dark bronze outside. Yellow flowers are sometimes damaged by sparrows.

Galanthus nivalis Y
Snowdrop

H and S 10cm/4in

Eagerly awaited, snowdrops help fill the slow weeks between midwinter and spring. Plants establish better when transplanted 'in the green', immediately after flowering, than from bulbs planted 8cm/3in deep during autumn (see pages 120–1).

POSITION In part shade and a humus-rich, well-drained soil. Good for colonizing banks and areas of sparse grass between trees.

MAINTENANCE Separate existing clumps and plant 15cm/6in apart to create a small carpet of plants.

ALTERNATIVES I love the simplicity of the common snowdrop, but there are many different species and cultivars to try. *G. n.* 'Flore Pleno' Y is a double form. *G.* 'S. Arnott' Y is particularly fine, with large, fragrant flowers with V-shaped, green markings at the tips of inner petals. The blooms of *G.* 'Magnet' Y are held out on long flower stalks.

Iris 'Cantab'

H 10–15cm/4–6in S 8cm/3in

Reticulata-type irises, among the first flowerers of late winter and early spring, naturalize well if undisturbed to form generous clumps blooming year after year. This paler blue variety shows up better against dark soils than deep-purple-coloured sorts. A good choice for rock gardens and containers.

POSITION In sun and ordinary, well-drained soil. Cover the slender bulbs with 5cm/2in of soil in groups

Iris 'Cantab'

ALTERNATIVES *L. regale* ♔, the regal lily, bears fragrant, trumpet-shaped, white flowers flushed with pink-purple outside in midsummer. *L.* 'Marco Polo' is similar to 'Casa Blanca' in shape and season, yet is a wonderful, shimmering sugar-pink.

Narcissus 'Jetfire' ♔
Daffodil

H 20cm/8in S 10cm/4in

Shorter daffodils are much easier to accommodate in gardens, especially in windswept areas. 'Jetfire' is yellow with a long orange trumpet and associates particularly well with the marble-leaved *Arum italicum* 'Marmoratum' (see page 135).

POSITION In sun or light shade in ordinary soils. Plant 10cm/4in deep, 10cm/4in apart in early autumn.

MAINTENANCE Make sure leaves remain on the plants for at least six weeks after flowering and never knot the foliage. Lift, separate and replant congested bulbs.

ALTERNATIVES *N.* 'Tête-à-Tête' is a bright yellow variety (see page 121),

12cm/5in apart (8cm/3in in pots) during autumn.

MAINTENANCE Note the location of bulbs so as not to damage or disturb them while weeding.

ALTERNATIVES Taller (60cm/24in) types for early summer are Dutch iris and moisture-loving English iris, *I. latifolia* ♔.

Lilium 'Casa Blanca' ♔
Lily

H 1–1.2m/3–4ft S 30cm/12in

There is something magical about white lilies (see pages 94–5). With *L. auratum* (the golden-rayed lily of

Japan) as a parent, this is a stunner. The fragrant, bowl-shaped flowers are pure white with orange stamens and open from long buds in mid- to late summer. They follow on nicely from the widely planted *L. regale*.

POSITION In full sun or part shade. Plant during autumn or spring, setting the bulbs a good 15cm/6in deep and 30cm/12in apart. In pots, set three bulbs to a 30cm/12in pot.

MAINTENANCE When growth starts, push some twig supports into the pot or soil around the plants. Water well and add liquid fertilizer every fortnight when pot-grown.

Narcissus 'Jetfire'

Nerine bowdenii

Scilla siberica

while *N*. 'Jack Snipe' ♈, also 20cm/8in tall, bears a more subtle white flower with yellow trumpet. At 40cm/16in high, *N*. 'Ice Follies' ♈ is taller but because the white flowers are neat the plants are sturdier.

Nerine bowdenii ♈
H 45cm/18in S 23cm/9in

Pink, lily-like flowers are carried on naked stalks during autumn; the leaves appear separately during spring. Nerine associates well with most other autumn flowers including the purples and blues of Michaelmas daisies or the hazy blue of *Caryopteris* x *clandonensis*.

POSITION In sun and well-drained soil. Plant new bulbs in early spring, with their necks just visible.

MAINTENANCE Lift, divide and replant existing clumps when in leaf.

ALTERNATIVE *Amaryllis belladonna* also bears naked flower stalks during autumn, but the pink blooms are larger and held taller.

Scilla siberica ♈
Siberian squill

H 10–15cm/4–6in S 8cm/3in

An initial sprinkling of pendent, bright blue spring flowers will, over the years, naturalize and spread into a fine colony. Suits a rock garden, gravel area or under deciduous trees.

POSITION In sun or part shade in ordinary soils. Plant bulbs 8cm/3in deep and 8–10cm/3–4in apart in early autumn.

MAINTENANCE Avoid disturbing soil around the bulbs when weeding. For wider colonies, lift, divide and replant clumps after flowering.

ALTERNATIVE For pools of starry, light blue flowers around the bases of shrubs, plant *S. mischtschenkoana,* which does well even in shade.

Tulipa 'High Society'
Tulip

H 35cm/14in S 15cm/6in

Tulips are the easiest bulbs to add among existing plants in borders or pots in autumn. This one opens its glowing mango, pink and red flowers in mid-spring (see pages 80–1).

POSITION In sun and good, well-drained soil. Plant tulips in late autumn, tucking them, 13cm/5in deep, between existing plants.

MAINTENANCE I lift my tulips, to prevent a hotchpotch from previous years spoiling my planned display. Bulbs can be dried and stored for summer, then planted into good soil in autumn for cut flowers.

ALTERNATIVES *T*. 'Spring Green' ♈ is 50cm/20in high with green markings on the back of its white petals, and slightly shorter 'Apricot Beauty' is a soft apricot colour. At 60cm/24in, 'Queen of Night' is dark maroon. For a short (20cm/8in), fun tulip, 'Johann Strauss' bears long, fluted yellow flowers with a red mark on each petal. For pink, the species *T. saxatilis* has mauve-pink flowers with yellow centres, grows to 20cm/8in high and naturalizes well.

Argyranthemum 'Cornish Gold' ♔

Marguerite

H and **S** 60cm/24in

A compact, shrubby plant with attractive foliage and a succession of 5cm/2in-wide yellow daisy flowers from early summer to autumn. Ideal for filling gaps (three plants easily fill a square metre) or in large pots (see pages 108–9).

POSITION Sun and well-drained soil.

MAINTENANCE No staking required. Deadheading is not essential as new flowers will still keep coming. Plants are frost tender and can be dug out and composted in autumn. Over-wintering and propagation is best left to those with more time.

ALTERNATIVES *A.* 'Jamaica Primrose' grows taller and is more likely to swamp existing plants. *A.* 'Summer Stars' is more compact, with small pink anemone-style flowers.

Canna 'Wyoming'

Indian shot

H 1.2–1.8m/4–6ft **S** 50cm/20in

More and more gardeners are catching on to the impressive display provided by cannas. New growth starts in spring from rhizomes and develops throughout summer, with flowers appearing from midsummer to early autumn. This one boasts brown-purple leaves with darker veins and bright orange flowers (see page 116).

POSITION In sun; the more fertile the soil and the more attention paid to watering and feeding, the bigger and bolder a canna will grow.

MAINTENANCE In mild areas of light frost, cannas can be left in the soil; a mulch over the top will insulate them. Elsewhere, lift in autumn, pot up and keep almost dry until spring.

ALTERNATIVES *C.* 'Black Knight' bears bronze leaves and dark red flowers. For smaller, well-spaced yellow and warm salmon flowers against dark green foliage, try *C.* 'Panache'.

Dahlia 'Bishop of Llandaff' ♔

H 1m/40in **S** 60cm/24in

Surely the most popular of dahlias, it is one of the easiest to assimilate into a border with other plants. Bright red, semi-double flowers with darker centres complement the metallic foliage perfectly (see page 116).

POSITION In sun; dahlias need well-cultivated, fertile, moist yet well-drained soil to give of their best.

MAINTENANCE Plant tubers in spring, setting them 10cm/4in deep, or buy

***Dahlia* 'Bishop of Llandaff'**

plants in pots and plant out in early summer. In areas where frosts are light and short, leave in the ground. Elsewhere, lift, dry off and store in a frost-free place with some dry compost over their roots.

ALTERNATIVES Free-branching *D.* 'Chimborazo' (1.2m/4ft high) bears attractive red outer petals surrounding a yellow inner collar. *D.* 'David Howard' bears dark-centred, double orange flowers against bronze foliage (1–1.5m/3–5ft high).

Digitalis purpurea ♔

Foxglove

H 1–2m/3–6ft **S** 60cm/24in

Spires of tubular bell-shaped flowers are purple-pink or white and spotted inside. Foxgloves are excellent gap-fillers, adding a wild touch to the garden. As biennials, they are sown in spring or bought in during summer and autumn so that first-year plants can be established during autumn. Large rosettes of leaves will rise up to flower the following summer (see pages 14–15).

POSITION In sun or part shade, in well-drained soil.

MAINTENANCE Cut away main spike after flowering and smaller spikes will follow. Leave some seed pods to ripen and self-seed.

ALTERNATIVES *D.* Excelsior Group ♔ is a seed mixture yielding plants with flowers of cream, white, yellow, pink and purple. For white flowers only, choose *D. p.* f. *albiflora* ♔. Unusual *D. parviflora* is grown for its architectural, 60cm/2ft-high spires of small orange-brown flowers.

Gazania 'Talent' ♛

H 20cm/8in **S** 25cm/10in

Plant in early summer where sun will coax its large, brightly coloured, rosette-like daisy flowers open until well into autumn, revealing petals that can be exquisitely patterned. A sturdy and drought-tolerant plant.

POSITION Sun and hot, dry conditions bring out the best in gazanias. Light, well-drained soil is ideal and plants flourish in dry, shingle-topped beds.

MAINTENANCE Deadheading is not essential. In mild areas, leave plants in for the winter as they sometimes sprout again in spring.

ALTERNATIVE *G.* 'Kiss' is more compact and keeps its flowers open longer under cool, dull conditions than some other gazanias.

Lathyrus odoratus 'Wiltshire Ripple' ♛

Sweet pea

H 2–2.5m/6–8ft

This is just one of many cultivars of the frilly-petalled, fragrant Spencer sweet peas. Buy and grow a mixture to enjoy a variety of jewel-like colours. Growing options include spring sowings into the soil, sowing into pots followed by planting out, or buying young plants. Sweet peas have a limited flowering period, but planting in mid-spring and early summer ensures a longer season.

POSITION In sun or part shade and good rich soil. I usually fix up my wigwam of hazel or willow poles, then either sow or plant around it.

MAINTENANCE Water in well, keep moist and take steps to control slugs (see page 168). Apply a couple of doses of liquid fertilizer during

Lathyrus odoratus 'Wiltshire Ripple'

growth. Pick the flowers regularly or deadhead rigorously to encourage more buds.

ALTERNATIVES The original sweet pea *L. odoratus* is smaller-growing than the Spencer cultivars, and bears two to four wine-red and purple flowers on each stem. Very fragrant, it blends well with *Pennisetum alopecuroides* (fountain grass) (see page 133).

Lunaria annua

Honesty

H 60-90cm/24-36in **S** 30cm/12in

Once introduced, honesty becomes semi-wild and self-seeds freely. Sow this biennial in spring, or buy plants to establish in autumn for purple flowers in late spring the following year. Flat seed pods follow, which turn silvery and transparent, lasting well into winter (see pages 118–9).

POSITION In sun or part shade and well-drained (even poor, dry) soil.

MAINTENANCE Thin out seedlings. Do not cut back after flowering, as this would remove seedheads, which are great winter features.

ALTERNATIVES *L. a.* 'Variegata' has leaves margined and marked creamy white and bears a lively show of red-purple flowers (see page 16). *L. a.* var. *albiflora* ♛ has white flowers.

Nicotiana alata

Tobacco plant

H 60–120cm/2–4ft **S** 30cm/12in

A white-flowered, old-fashioned annual, full of character and fragrance. Its shy flowers are closed by day which makes their evening performance all the more special (see pages 94–5). Finding seeds or plants is becoming something of a challenge.

POSITION In sun or part shade. Prefers moist but well-drained soil, but tolerates poor dry soils well. Use to fill gaps in borders.

MAINTENANCE Water to settle new plants in. No need to deadhead.

ALTERNATIVES Taller *N. sylvestris* ♛ has tubular flowers but with less pervasive perfume. *N. langsdorffii* ♛, shorter, has small jade-green flowers.

Nigella damascena 'Miss Jekyll'

Nigella damascena
Love-in-a-mist

H to 50cm/20in S to 23cm/9in

Sow this hardy annual straight into the ground in spring. Thin seedlings to about 13cm/5in apart for a patch of delightful filigree plants topped by blue flowers on a ruff of foliage (see page 25). *N. d.* 'Miss Jekyll' has lovely sky-blue flowers.

POSITION Sun and well-drained soil.

MAINTENANCE Push twiggy sticks in the soil at low angles to protect seed from the digging and rolling of cats. Leave the attractive seedheads for interest and because they self-seed.

ALTERNATIVES For a wider colour range, the Persian Jewel Series offers both sky and deep blue, and pale and deep pink or white flowers.

Petunia (Ultra Series) 'Ultra Rose Star'

H 25–30cm/10–12in S to 60cm/24in

Buy petunias to plant out in early summer. The Ultra Series make billowing plants bearing large, but reasonably weather-resistant flowers all summer. Set 23cm/9in apart to fill gaps in borders. This stripy sort is great fun and adds a festive, seaside holiday effect to any border.

POSITION In sun and good, but well-drained soil.

MAINTENANCE Protect young plants from slugs (see page 168) and apply a couple of well-balanced liquid feeds as they grow. Deadheading is desirable. In autumn pull up plants.

ALTERNATIVES There are many kinds of petunia, but stick to plants of one colour when using them as summer fillers in borders (see pages 94–5). Pale pink cultivars look great against silvery plants such as artemisias.

Rudbeckia hirta 'Rustic Dwarfs'

Rudbeckia hirta 'Rustic Dwarfs'
Coneflower

H 60cm/24in S 25cm/10in

Reliable and easy to grow, flowers are a satisfying blend of gold, bronze and red with dark cones produced all summer and into autumn. The main planting time is late spring, but they make excellent midsummer gap-fillers where perennials have died off, providing extra colour where needed.

POSITION In sun or part shade; suits most soils including poor, dry ones.

MAINTENANCE Water in and while establishing. Pull up in autumn.

ALTERNATIVES *R. h.* 'Goldilocks' has dark-centred double golden flowers, and 'Marmalade' (see pages 100–1) produces large double or semi-double golden-orange flowerheads.

Verbascum bombyciferum ♔
Mullein

H 1.2–1.8m/4–6ft S 60cm/24in

Sow seed in early summer, or buy plants to establish by autumn. At first this biennial's beauty lies in large rosettes of silvery, woolly foliage brightening winter gardens. Then in the following summer, spikes of sulphur-yellow flowers rise.

POSITION Sun and poor, well-drained soil produce the best results.

MAINTENANCE Allow plants to seed, then avoid soil disturbance to allow this beautiful plant to naturalize in the garden. Move seedlings to better positions while small. Should plants lean, prop up with twiggy sticks.

ALTERNATIVES *V.* 'Snow Maiden', a perennial at 1.2m/4ft, has white flowers. Dainty yellow-flowered *V. chaixii* 'Gainsborough' ♔ (below) is a stronger perennial than some.

Verbascum chaixii 'Gainsborough'

Allium schoenoprasum

Chives

H 45cm/18in S 23cm/9in

Easy to grow and use: snip off young leaves (preferably), chop and sprinkle on to new potatoes and salads or in cream cheese. Small but attractive, globular mauve flower heads appear in summer. Plants die back for winter. Looks good as an edging plant or divider.

POSITION In sun and rich, moist, but well-drained soil.

MAINTENANCE As leaves toughen, cut them all back to within 2.5cm/1in of the ground, and repeat this tactic as necessary unless you want flowers to form. Clumps are easy to lift, split and replant during spring.

ALTERNATIVES Choose *A. s.* fine-leaved form for its useful, delicate foliage. For white flowers, choose *A. s.* white form. *A. tuberosum* (garlic chives) is also white-flowered and has flattish, garlic-flavoured leaves.

Courgette

H and S 90cm/36in

Plant or sow in late spring or early summer (see pages 102–3), towards the fronts of borders to fill large gaps. Yellow flowers are followed by green or yellow fruits. Crop these regularly to encourage more. Compost plants in autumn. Associates well with parsley, which will revel in the shade of its foliage.

POSITION Sun and moist, fertile soil.

MAINTENANCE Water during dry periods and apply fertilizer on poor soils. Protect young plants from slugs and snails (see page 168).

ALTERNATIVES Squash can be grown in much the same way, as can marrows and pumpkins, but these last two require much more space.

Runner bean 'Hestia'

H 45–60cm/18–24in S 15cm/6in

Instead of filling border gaps with bedding plants, sow bush runner beans such as this one or dwarf green beans in late spring. They have attractive flowers and will provide crops of beans better and fresher than any you can buy – the French filet type are good because they are expensive to buy. Make parallel drills 5cm/2in deep and sow 8cm/3in apart (see page 24).

POSITION In sun and good, moist, but well-drained soil.

MAINTENANCE Protect young seedlings from slugs and snails (see page 168). Plants toughen up and become less vulnerable when older. Water during droughts, especially when flowers are setting. Pick regularly to encourage more flowers and beans. No supports are needed.

ALTERNATIVES 'Pickwick', a bush runner bean, needs no support. Try also dwarf French bean 'Delinel' or pencil-podded bean 'Safari'.

Rosmarinus officinalis 'Primley Blue'

Rosemary

H and S 1.5m/5ft

Incorporating rosemary into a shrub planting adds evergreen, aromatic foliage with long-lasting flowers as well as a useful culinary herb. This cultivar bears intensely blue flowers

Runner bean 'Hestia'

from spring to summer, then again in autumn. It is a joy to be able to nip off sprigs of the needle-like foliage for cooking (especially good with roast lamb) at any time of the year. Rosemary is a good container plant, too, where constant cropping will result in compact plants.

POSITION A sunny, sheltered spot in well-drained soil. It can be used to create a low, informal hedge.

MAINTENANCE Trim or give a more regenerative prune in spring.

ALTERNATIVES *R. o.* 'Miss Jessopp's Upright' bears pale blue flowers and is particularly good for hedging. *R. o.* 'Roseus' bears pink flowers.

Salvia officinalis

Common sage

H and S 75cm/30in

Like rosemary and thyme, sage is a stalwart among culinary herbs, its evergreen nature providing winter pickings. A small shrub, it has grey-green leaves netted by small veins into tiny cushions. If not picked or cut back, shoots will terminate in attractive spikes of blue flowers in summer.

POSITION In sun and well-drained soil. Tolerates poor, sandy soils well.

MAINTENANCE To keep plants neat, prune (though not into old wood) in spring or after flowering.

ALTERNATIVES There are coloured-leaved varieties just as useful for cooking. The dusky purple foliage of *S. o.* Purpurascens Group looks wonderful with pink roses. *S. o.* 'Icterina' ♥, gold sage, has gold edges to the leaves and *S. o.* 'Tricolor' shows pink flushes on its newer, cream-edged leaves.

Salad rocket

H 25cm/10in S 17cm/7in

The half-hour gardener has little time to deal with lettuce, but here is an easy salad crop capable of yielding pickings over a long period. It is pleasant on its own, or the leaves add bite to more mundane salads. Sow in parallel drills 20cm/8in apart in spring and thin to 8cm/3in. Sow again in early autumn.

POSITION In light shade and a fertile, moist soil.

MAINTENANCE Leaves rather than whole plants are picked and this must be done regularly to prevent plants from running up to flower.

ALTERNATIVES Stronger-tasting wild rocket is worth a try. Red cos lettuce harvested young is a good addition to salads, and slugs tend to avoid it.

Sweet corn

H 1.2m/4ft S 60cm/24in

Block-planting this ornamental in the border looks stylish and ensures a good set of corn on the cob.

POSITION A warm, sunny sheltered site and moist, fertile soil. Set plants 38cm/15in apart (see page 102).

MAINTENANCE Protect young plants from slugs (see page 168) and water in dry periods.

ALTERNATIVES All cultivars on sale will give good results.

Thymus vulgaris

Common garden thyme

H 30cm/12in S 24cm/9in

When crushed, the foliage of this thyme releases a mouthwatering fragrance. Easily raised from seed, small plants quickly grow into low, spreading shrubs. Harvest often to keep plants compact. Summer flowers are mauve.

POSITION In sun or light shade, and a well-drained soil. Plants will straggle in too much shade. Makes a great path edging, where trodden leaves release their aroma.

MAINTENANCE A light shearing over plants in spring or after flowering helps keep them compact.

ALTERNATIVES Silver-edged *T. v.* 'Silver Posie' and gold-leaved *T. v.* 'Goldentiné (syn. *T. v* 'Aureus') make attractive variations. Lemon thyme (*T. x citriodorus*) makes a good mound-like shape and its piquant flavour is good to cook with. Silvery and gold-leaved cultivars are available.

Tomato 'Sweet 100'

Tomato 'Sweet 100'

H 1.2m/4ft S 60cm/24in

Home-grown tomatoes ripened in the sun and picked straight from the plant have unrivalled flavour. This is a cherry type tomato and just one or two, planted 60–75cm/24–30in apart in borders in early summer, will produce plenty of sweet fruit. Provide each with a stake and nip out sideshoots to restrict growth. Stop the tip after four or five trusses have formed. The easiest tomatoes are smaller bush types which need no staking or pinching out.

POSITION In sun in good, fertile soil.

MAINTENANCE Weed around the plants. Water during dry periods. Apply a liquid tomato fertilizer once a week when flowers start forming.

ALTERNATIVES You will have to be guided by what plants are for sale at the garden centre. Look out for 'Carefree' and 'Red Alert' for beds and 'Tumbler' for containers.

vegetables and herbs

Note: though not strictly grasses, bamboos are included here.

Asplenium scolopendrium ♔
Hart's tongue fern
H 45–60cm/18–24in S 60cm/24in
Though this fern is described as evergreen, its main interest is from spring to autumn. Fronds unfurl, fresh and vibrant, in spring, to strap-shaped but pointed, glossy green tongues. An invaluable fern for adding romance to weed-cleared shady corners with other wild, but

Matteuccia struthiopteris

pretty plants (see page 90). Spreads by spores, but never invasively.
POSITION In light or deep shade. Moist but well-drained soil is best, but short dry periods are tolerated.
MAINTENANCE Remove old, dead fronds, especially in spring.
ALTERNATIVES All hardy ferns are pretty, but none has the same freshness and impact. Those with good leaf variations include *A. s.* (Crispum Group) 'Crispum Bolton's Nobile' ♔ with wavy margins.

Chusquea culeou ♔
H 1.8–6m/6–20ft S 2.5m/8ft or more
A graceful bamboo which, though slow to establish, eventually makes a majestic clump of canes in varying shades of yellow and olive green. Persistent, tapering, pale and papery leaf sheaths on young canes are hallmarks, as are its unusual solid stems. Branches grow out of the nodes in clusters, bearing the leaves.
POSITION Likes a sheltered position in sun or part shade on good, moist but well-drained soil.
MAINTENANCE For thick clumps, leave well alone. For a structural effect, thin weak or badly placed canes. Young plants can be moved, but can take a year or two to settle.
ALTERNATIVE For smaller gardens, try *C. c.* 'Tenuis' (1.2–1.5m/4–5ft high).

Festuca gautieri
H 25cm/10in S 30cm/12in
Makes attractive wide hummocks of dense moss-green leaves, which look needle-like yet are soft to the touch.

Small pale green flowers appear in summer, but this evergreen grass is grown more for its year-round structure. Most effective when planted in a group of three, five or seven, spaced 30cm/12in apart.
POSITION In sun; thrives best in dry, not too fertile soils, so it is ideal for poor, sandy soil.
MAINTENANCE Snatch out dead foliage from time to time. Ants' nests under the roots can undermine the plant by forcing it upwards.
ALTERNATIVES *F. glauca* 'Golden Toupee' and 'Elijah Blue' and 'Blaufuchs' (see pages 98–9) make smaller, sparser hummocks with colours true to their names.

Matteuccia struthiopteris ♔
Shuttlecock fern
H 90cm/3ft S 75cm/30in
A most shapely fern. In spring newly emerging fronds are like 'shuttlecocks', maturing to graceful bright green sterile fronds which arch outwards as they age. Shorter, brown, spore-bearing fronds appear in the centre of each cluster. Interplant with hostas, Siberian iris and rhododendrons or, for a classy look, with ground cover or swathes of white impatiens.
POSITION In part shade in humus-rich, moist but well-drained, neutral to acid soil.
MAINTENANCE Each fern spreads by rhizomes to form a colony, but is not invasive. Dies back in winter, but leave dead fronds in place to protect the crowns. A moisture-holding mulch helps lush growth.

Pennisetum alopecuroides 'Hameln'

Pennisetum alopecuroides 'Hameln'
Fountain grass
H 90cm/3ft S 75cm/30in

A classic grass with presence, which is easily accommodated in borders alongside shrubs and perennials. Though it is evergreen, old foliage looks wintry until new growth pushes its way through in spring, arching into attractive mounds. Stalks bearing shimmering brownish spikelets are held out beyond the foliage from summer through to winter. They are seen at their best in low shafts of autumnal light.

POSITION In sun; suits well-drained soils of poor to average fertility, and also poor, sandy soils.

MAINTENANCE Trim back older foliage just before new growth in early spring. Lift and divide to increase clumps during late spring.

ALTERNATIVE *P. orientale* ♔ is grown for its pink spikelets (60cm/24in high).

Phyllostachys aureosulcata 'Spectabilis'
Yellow-groove bamboo
H 3.7m/12ft S indefinite

A choice tall, yet dainty bamboo with branches of leaves held out on all sides. Its prettily coloured canes are gold striped with green and suffused with pink.

POSITION In sun or dappled shade. Fertile, moist soil is best, but grows in poor sandy soils and also heavier ones. Good for large containers.

MAINTENANCE Allow to thicken into dense clumps. To improve structure and for clean, visible canes, remove bottom side-branches, thin out weedy or badly placed canes and dig out any threatening to invade other plants. Not especially rampant, but like all bamboos it needs watching.

ALTERNATIVE *P. nigra* ♔, similar in habit, has striking black canes.

Polystichum setiferum ♔
Soft shield fern
H 75cm/30in S 90cm/3ft

Young fronds unfurl like octopus tentacles, bright green against darker old fronds. Once they have expanded, the overall effect is of mossy, radiating fronds, as the pinnae (fern leaves) divide, then divide again (becoming bipinnate).

POSITION In shade or part shade. Humus-rich, well-drained soil is ideal, but this fern is a gift for dry, shaded places.

MAINTENANCE Divide large, multi-crowned clumps in spring. Push the tiny plantlets on mature fronds into pots of compost to root.

ALTERNATIVES Several cultivars include those with complicated, more densely divided pinnae. The

Stipa gigantea

eyelashed fern, *P. polyblepharum*, is covered with golden hairs.

Stipa gigantea
Giant feather grass
H 1.8m/6ft S 1.5m/5ft

Though tall, this stipa is easy to slot in among other plants; it looks good with shrub roses and dwarf pines like *Pines mugo*. A clump of narrow, dark green leaves only 75cm/30in high is topped in early summer by long stems with oat-flower sprays that move beautifully in breezes.

POSITION In sun or part shade and average, well-drained soil; tolerates poor, sandy soil well.

MAINTENANCE Tidy up older leaves of this semi-evergreen in early spring before new growth appears. Should clumps need splitting, do so in late spring or early summer.

ALTERNATIVE No other grass is as stately, but *S. tenuissima* (60cm/2ft high) creates a sea of feathery flower spikes in summer (see pages 98–9).

grasses and ferns

Acanthus mollis
Bear's breeches

H to 1.2m/4ft **S** to 90cm/36in

The handsome evergreen lobed leaves of this native of south-west Europe and north-west Africa may look familiar, for they have long been the inspiration for ornament on classical columns. In summer tall spires of white tubular flowers grow from purple bracts to striking effect, especially when plants are allowed to develop into large clumps and repeated several times in a garden.

POSITION In sun or part shade; they tolerate poor soils, but grow best in moist, fertile soil.

MAINTENANCE Should more plants be needed, lift, divide and replant clumps in autumn or spring.

ALTERNATIVE An equally resilient performer, *A. spinosus* ♛ has narrower, more divided, almost spiny leaves.

Alchemilla mollis

Alchemilla mollis
Lady's mantle

H 30–60cm/12–24in **S** 50cm/30in

In spring beautifully lobed, softly hairy pale green leaves appear, noted for the beads of water that decorate their leaf edges in the morning. A haze of tiny greenish-yellow flowers follows from early summer to autumn, when plants slowly die back for winter.

POSITION In sun or shade in any soil, but soil quality dictates size. Makes excellent ground cover that is impenetrable to weeds, and self-seeds freely.

MAINTENANCE Shear back dying flower stems for an autumn tidy-up.

ALTERNATIVE *A. fulgens* is similar, but smaller in every way, reaching only 30cm/12in.

Anemone hupehensis 'Splendens'
Windflower

H 60–90cm/2–3ft **S** 40cm/16in

The taller, late-flowering anemones from Japan and China – earning the name windflower as their pink or white blooms sway on long stems – are useful border plants, producing large flowers from midsummer to autumn when much else dies back. *A. hupehensis* and its cultivars start flowering in midsummer, soon joined by the cultivars of *A. x hybrida*, known as Japanese anemones. All die back for winter.

POSITION In sun or part shade and a moist, fertile soil.

MAINTENANCE Plants need little attention and are self-supporting,

Anemone hupehensis 'Splendens'

unless on thin, dry soils. Long woody tap roots make moving difficult, so they are best left in clumps.

ALTERNATIVES For height (1.2m/4ft) and later flowers, choose cultivars of *A. x hybrida* such as glorious white-flowered 'Honorine Jobert' ♛, whose blooms glow at dusk, or pink-flowered *A. x h.* 'Elegans' *(syn. A. x h.* 'Max Vogel').

Anthemis tinctoria 'Sauce Hollandaise'
Yellow chamomile

H and **S** 60cm/24in

Cream-coloured, daisy-like flowers are held above a backdrop of grey-

easy-care plants

green, fern-like foliage, evergreen and aromatic. The flowers last for several weeks during summer.

POSITION In sun on average soils. On rich, moist soils, they can reach 90cm/3ft but will thrive well and are at their most compact on poor, thin, sandy soils.

MAINTENANCE Shear back after the first flush of flowers and another will appear. Shear again at the end of the season, to maintain a dense, bushy plant. Staking not required.

ALTERNATIVES *A. t.* 'E. C. Buxton' and *A.t.* 'Wargrave Variety' both produce clouds of pale yellow daisies.

Aquilegia vulgaris var. *stellata* 'Firewheel'

Columbine, granny's bonnets

H 60–90cm/2–3ft **S** 45cm/18in

Aquilegias are up there with roses and iris at the top of my list of must-have flowers. They are very variable, making a mound of attractive, blue-green, lobed leaves then single or double purple, blue,

Aquilegia 'Firewheel'

pink or white spurred flowers in late spring (see pages 88–9). 'Firewheel', a clematis-flowered, spurless type with pink blooms, is one to try.

POSITION In sun or light shade. They prefer moist, fertile, but well-drained soils, but tolerate poor, dry soils well.

MAINTENANCE Plants self-seed in a useful, non-invasive way and can be introduced by seed sown into the borders in autumn or spring.

ALTERNATIVES *A. alpina* reaches 45cm/18in and bears deep blue flowers. The flashy *A. McKana* Group and other hybrids bear larger flowers in all the colours of the rainbow with very long spurs.

Arum italicum 'Marmoratum' ♡

Lords and ladies

H 30cm/12in **S** 20cm/8in

Glossy, arrow-shaped leaves, marbled with pale green or cream over the veins, provide valuable winter foliage. Leaves thrust through the ground in autumn and although appearing to wither in frosts, they spring back magically after a thaw. They reach their tallest in spring, then produce pale flower spathes followed by spikes of orange-red berries as the leaves die back for summer.

POSITION In sun or shade. A fertile, moist soil is best, but plants will grow in poor, dry soils too. Plant with small daffodils under deciduous shrubs.

MAINTENANCE Remove the red berries if children use the garden, because, like the rest of the plant, they are poisonous.

ALTERNATIVES None matches in value.

Arum italicum 'Marmoratum'

Astrantia major 'Hadspen Blood'

Hattie's pincushion

H 30–90cm/1–3ft **S** 45cm/18in

From the carrot and cow parsley family, these understated yet useful perennials have a simplicity and grace. They bear sprays of neat, rounded flower umbels, each surrounded by a ruff of bracts, which blend well with other plants. This variety has dark red tiny flowers and bracts.

POSITION In sun or part shade. Astrantias must be planted in a moist, humus-rich soil if they are to thrive.

MAINTENANCE Lift and divide large clumps in autumn or spring (see pages 34–5) to repeat the airy effect of the flowers along a border.

ALTERNATIVES For a cultivar with white flowers and bracts choose *A. m.* subsp. *involucrata* 'Shaggy'. *A. m.* 'Sunningdale Variegated' ♡ has pink flowers and leaves edged irregularly with cream and yellow.

hardy perennials

Bergenia 'Sunningdale'
Elephant's ears

H 30–45cm/12–18in **S** 60cm/2ft

Bold, evergreen foliage stands out in winter, when much else has died back to twigs and crowns. The cabbage-like leaves, though green during summer, turn coppery-red during winter, particularly in good light and following cold weather. Richly coloured, lilac-pink flowers appear on stout stems during spring.

POSITION In sun or shade. Bergenias grow bigger in moist, fertile soil, but can tolerate poorer, drier soils. Being structured plants, they look good in formal town gardens and are useful for difficult spots under trees.

MAINTENANCE Remove dead leaves from time to time.

ALTERNATIVES For white flowers, choose _B._ 'Bressingham White' ♈. Those of _B._ 'Silberlicht' ♈ are pale pink, and for deep pinkish-red, opt for _B._ 'Morgenröte'.

Echinops ritro 'Veitch's Blue'
Globe thistle

H 90cm/36in **S** 45cm/18in

Stiff and stately, echinops usually stand well to attention with the minimum of staking. Thistle-like, spiny leaves are lightly felted and make a good green-grey contrast to the bright blue flowers packed tightly into spherical heads. Beloved of bees, these appear during mid- to late summer and make bold border statements and good cut flowers.

POSITION In sun or part shade. It needs a well-drained soil and tolerates poor, dry soils.

MAINTENANCE Should stems lean, prop up with twiggy sticks. Divide large clumps in spring or autumn.

Echinacea purpurea with _Sidalcea malviflora_ 'Elsie Heugh' behind

ALTERNATIVE _E. bannaticus_ 'Taplow Blue' ♈ is similar.

Echinacea purpurea
Purple coneflower

H 60–90cm/2–3ft **S** 45cm/18in

Magnificent daisy-like flowers up to 12cm/5in across open from midsummer to autumn. Each bears bright pink petals surrounding a raised, orange central cone.

POSITION In sun; fertile well-drained soil gives best results, but poor, dry soils are tolerated. Excellent in a swathe for spreading through the front to middle sections of a border, and associates really well with plants such as ornamental grasses and _Sedum spectabile._

MAINTENANCE Remove dead stems when they become brown and soggy in mid-winter. Avoid disturbance to the roots when weeding.

ALTERNATIVES _E. p._ 'Magnus' bears a wider, flatter flower. The less showy, creamy flowerheads of _E. p._ 'White Lustre' blend well with the pink.

Eryngium x oliverianum ♈
Sea holly

H 90cm/36in **S** 45cm/18in

Of great architectural appeal, these metallic-leaved wonders bear spiny foliage and, from midsummer to early autumn, branched stems bearing umbels of small flowers in thimble-shaped domes, each of which sits on a wide collar of silvery, purple-blue, spiny bracts.

POSITION In sun; suits a poor, well-drained soil, and hates soggy roots in winter.

MAINTENANCE Use twiggy sticks to support flopping flower stems.

ALTERNATIVES _E. alpinum_ ♈, a parent of the above, is smaller in all respects, with a dainty, steely-blue, ethereal appearance. The other parent, _E. giganteum_ ♈ (Miss Willmott's ghost), H 90cm/36in, bears flowerheads surrounded by wide silvery bracts, Usually treated as a biennial, it self-seeds freely.

Euphorbia characias subsp. wulfenii ♈
Spurge

H and **S** 1.2m/4ft

The contrast between deep green, linear leaves and acid yellow/lime green flowerheads is a great feature of spring. On closer inspection, the 'flowers' consist of bracts enclosing the flower structure inside. These plants make stately bushes which look especially good teamed with purple and silver foliage and purple flowers like alliums.

POSITION In sun and well-drained soil; euphorbias also tolerate poor, dry soils.

MAINTENANCE Once the flowers have faded by summer, cut the flowered stems down to encourage new growth. Protect skin against sap, which can irritate.

ALTERNATIVES *E. characias* is similar with dark nectar glands on the flowers. *E.* × *martinii* ♔ is smaller at 90cm/3ft. For ground cover, *E. amygdaloides* var. *robbiae* (Mrs Robb's bonnet) reaches 60cm/24in and spreads nicely (see pages 82–3). *E. polychroma* makes mounds of pale green at 40cm/16in high.

Geranium psilostemon ♔
Armenian cranesbill
H and **S** 60–90cm/24–36in

A splendid geranium which grows into a significant plant with large-lobed leaves and, all summer, a profusion of shocking, magenta-pink flowers with black centres. There is nothing wispy about this plant, which fills gaps really well. Leaves turn red in autumn.

POSITION In sun or part shade. Geraniums suit most soils, as long as they are well drained.

MAINTENANCE Like most hardy geraniums, this one is adept at taking care of itself.

ALTERNATIVES *G. sanguineum*, the bloody cranesbill, another good gap-filler, will on a good soil reach 45cm/18in in height (if supported) and spread. Its magenta with white-centred flowers, produced all summer, look good with the pale pink of *G. s.* var. *striatum*.

Helleborus argutifolius ♔
Corsican hellebore
H 1.2m/4ft **S** 90cm/36in

Strong evergreen foliage plants for winter are valuable assets and this hellebore is one of the best. Tough

Geranium psilostemon

stems bear large, blue-green, almost silvery leaves, each divided into three toothed leaflets, and joined in late winter by an eruption of pale buds opening to pale green flowers.

POSITION In sun or light shade. This hellebore tolerates most soils whether light or heavy.

MAINTENANCE Stems tend to become heavy and flop, so either prop them up or leave them to look natural. Old stems can be cut away as new growth starts in spring.

ALTERNATIVES Nothing else has quite the same winter impact, but a group of common stinking hellebore (*H. foetidus* ♔) will offer striking winter foliage. Hellebores grown for their flowers include Christmas rose (*H. niger*), which looks best raised up in a container. Lenten hellebores (*H. hybridus*) are a promiscuous group with much flower variation including popular spotted and dark purple types. They prefer well-drained but moisture-retentive soil.

Helleborus argutifolius

Iris 'Alcazar'
Tall bearded iris

H 75cm/30in S 45cm/18in

Many of the numerous bearded iris cultivars bear a sweet perfume; some have particularly jewel-like colours. In size they range from the dwarf, late-spring-flowering kinds, through to the taller hybrids which open their flag-like flowers in early summer. Though the flowers are fleeting, the sword-like foliage adds structure from spring to autumn.

POSITION In sun and a well-drained soil; poor, dry soils are tolerated.

MAINTENANCE After several years the centre of a group dies out, leaving fans of growth concentrated around the outside. Lift in summer, cut away healthy rhizome portions with leaves attached and replant with the rhizomes at the surface. Leaves can be cut shorter for better stability.

ALTERNATIVES *I. pallida* 'Variegata' has cream-edged leaves and scented blue flowers with yellow beards. *I. sibirica*, Siberian iris, makes elegant clumps.

Iris 'Alcazar'

Knautia macedonica
Scabious

H 60cm/2ft S 45cm/18in

The small maroon flowers are arranged in exquisite pincushion-like heads held at the ends of long, strong, branching stems. Even without deadheading, flowers open from mid- to late summer. Neat rosettes of evergreen leaves remain close to the ground.

POSITION In sun or part shade in any well-drained soil. Looks great with yellow foliage plants like Bowles' golden grass (*Milium effusum* 'Aureum').

MAINTENANCE Cut back old flower stems in the autumn. Clumps expand gradually and continue to flower with little effort. Plants are easy to raise from seed.

ALTERNATIVE *Cirsium rivulare* 'Atropurpureum' is equally admired for its crimson-maroon thistle-like flowerheads capable of reaching 1.2m/4ft.

Kniphofia 'Percy's Pride'
Red hot poker

H 90cm/36in S 60cm/24in

Strictly speaking, this is a yellow hot poker, bearing flowers which are sulphur-yellow in bud, then turn creamier as they open fully. These are held aloft on stout stems which rise from tufts of narrow, pointed leaves during late summer. Most of the foliage dies back during winter.

POSITION In sun or part shade, and prefers rich, moist but well-drained soil. Clay is tolerated as long as water can drain away from it during winter. Repeated clumps in a border work well.

MAINTENANCE Cut back old flower

Knautia macedonica

stems in autumn. Clumps expand yearly and can be easily divided between autumn and spring.

ALTERNATIVES *K. caulescens* and *K. rooperi*, both reaching 1.2m/4ft, are taller and later-flowering (into autumn), and bear classic poker-like flowers where buds at the tip glow orange but open to yellow.

Lychnis coronaria
Rose campion, madam-pinch-me-quick

H 75cm/30in S 45cm/18in

Soft, silvery stems and leaves contrast with rounded, shocking pink flowers, though a subtler form bears pink-tinged, white flowers. Leaves make attractive silver rosettes during winter and then send up branching flower stems in summer.

POSITION In sun or part shade;

easy-care plants

Kniphofia with *Agapanthus* flowers

grows in normal, well-drained soil, and easily tolerates poor, dry soils.

MAINTENANCE Plants need little help and will usually self-seed around in a non-invasive way. Thin out unwanted seedlings (see page 49).

ALTERNATIVES *L. viscaria* (H/S 45cm/ 18in), the German catchfly or sticky Lizzie, makes clumps of narrow leaves and sticky stems of ragged-petalled pink flowers in early summer. *L. flos-jovis* is pretty in silver and pink.

Nepeta 'Six Hills Giant'
Catmint
H and **S** 90cm/36in
Expect bushy mounds of small, grey-green, aromatic leaves smothered in a haze of blue flowers for most of the summer. This catmint suits the cottage garden

style and is great for filling large gaps or edging pathways.

POSITION In sun or part shade in any well-drained soil.

MAINTENANCE Shear plants back after the first flush have flowers have faded and a fresh mass of growth and flowers will come. Cut old growth back in autumn if it is in the way, but give the plant a proper haircut in spring. Large plants can be chopped into several pieces during autumn or spring.

ALTERNATIVES *N.* x *faassenii* is similar but smaller (H/S 45cm/18in) if space is precious. Catnip or catnep, in particular *N. cataria,* attracts cats.

Papaver orientale 'Mrs Perry' ♀
Oriental poppy
H and **S** to 90cm/36in
It is hard to believe that plants with such enormous, fragile-looking flowers and silken petals are so easy to grow. A mass of hairy leaves in late spring and early summer is followed by flower stems with fat buds. This cultivar has blooms 12cm/ 5in across, and salmon-pink petals with black basal blotches. Petals fall to reveal fine, velvety seed pods shaped like bishops' caps.

POSITION In sun. Fertile, well-drained soil gives the best results.

MAINTENANCE Avoid overfeeding, which encourages floppy growth. Rain can cause mayhem, so support stems early on with twiggy sticks. The old stems die back naturally during summer, to be replaced with new growth by autumn. Make sure new leaves are not swamped by the foliage of other plants.

ALTERNATIVES The flowers of *P. o.*

Papaver orientale 'Mrs Perry'

Goliath Group 'Beauty of Livermere' ♀ are blood-red, those of *P . o.* 'Cedric Morris' ♀ pale pink.

Penstemon 'Evelyn' ♀
H 45–60cm/18–24in **S** 30cm/12in
Valued for their jewel-like colours during mid- to late summer, penstemons are justly popular. This cultivar is particularly dainty, making a bush of narrow leaves joined by a profusion of tubular rose-pink flowers with contrasting markings. Plants are semi-evergreen in mild areas.

POSITION In sun or part shade. Plants do well in ordinary, well-conditioned soil.

MAINTENANCE Cut away the stems which have finished flowering and more will be produced. Prune back dead growth in spring.

ALTERNATIVES This and most penstemons can tolerate freezing winter temperatures as long as their

hardy perennials

soil is well-drained. A few are not reliably frost hardy, so check when buying. *P.* 'Andenken an Friedrich Hahn' ♆ (sometimes called 'Garnet') is a good wine red, *P.* 'Appleblossom' ♆ is pink and white and *P. heterophyllus* bears a mist of dainty purple flowers.

Phlomis russeliana ♆

H 90cm/36in S 75cm/30in

This phlomis has a quiet structural beauty and makes useful ground cover for difficult shady places. Sage-green, heart-shaped leaves persist through winter and are joined throughout summer by tall stems bearing, at intervals, whorls of soft yellow, hooded flowers. The effect, of flowers or autumn seed-heads, is candelabra-like.

POSITION In sun or part shade, in any well-drained soil. Coming from Turkey, these plants, with hairy stems and leaves, tolerate drought.

MAINTENANCE No staking required. The dead stems can be left on the plants for an attractive winter outline. Cut back in spring. Divide plants in spring or collect and sow seed to obtain splendid soft yellow drifts useful to tie in plantings of shrubs and ground cover.

ALTERNATIVES *P. cashmeriana* bears hairier leaves and purple flowers. Shrubby phlomis like *P. fruticosa* are well worth investigating, too.

Phlox paniculata 'Eva Cullum'
Perennial phlox

H 1.2m/4ft S 60cm/24in

Good clumps of tall, self-supporting stems are capped with bright pink flowers centred with contrasting darker pink. This lightly fragrant

Rudbeckia fulgida var. *sullivantii* '*Goldsturm*'

display continues for several weeks from mid- to late summer, filling a useful gap. Phlox makes an excellent cut flower.

POSITION In sun or light shade. This type, *P. paniculata,* and its cultivars (unlike alpine types) need a moist, well-nourished soil to achieve their full potential, so avoid competition from nearby trees and hedges.

MAINTENANCE Apply a bucket of water to the roots during droughts. Large clumps can be lifted and divided during autumn.

ALTERNATIVES *P. p.* 'Graf Zeppelin' bears white flowers centred with pink. Those of *P . p.* 'Fujiyama' ♆ are also white.

Pulmonaria saccharata 'Leopard'
Lungwort, soldiers and sailors

H 30cm/12in S 45cm/18in

Lungworts are one of the joys of early spring. Almost before their new foliage has had a chance to sprout, clusters of buds open to jewel-like

flowers of purple-blue, changing to pink. Those of this cultivar are pinkish-red. Gradually, the leaves expand and become more spotted with silver, offering lush ground cover for the rest of the summer.

POSITION In shade or part shade. Plants grow best in a moist, fertile yet well-drained soil. Repetition works well, so allow clumps to develop all over the garden. They associate well with hardy ferns.

MAINTENANCE Remove dead leaves periodically, especially when plants begin to flower. Divide clumps during autumn. Seedlings usually come up all over the place and although these will not be identical to their parents, they are usually worth keeping.

ALTERNATIVES *P. s.* 'Mrs Moon' offers classic pink buds and blue flowers. *P.* 'Sissinghurst White' ♆ is a classic of the spring border. *P. rubra* 'Redstart' bears pinkish red flowers. For flowers of intense blue, choose *P.* 'Mawson's Blue'.

easy-care plants

Rudbeckia fulgida var. sullivantii 'Goldsturm' ♔
Coneflower, black-eyed Susan
H 60cm/24in **S** 45cm/18in

Flowering, from late summer into autumn, in clumps bearing a succession of bold but dainty golden-yellow, daisy-like flowers, each centred with a dark, chocolate-brown cone. Valued for late opening when flowers are needed, in colours that suit the season.

POSITION In sun or part shade. They prefer moist, fertile soils ranging from light to heavy, but perform well on dry, sandy soil too. Massed plants look great among drifts of grasses (see pages 2–3).

MAINTENANCE Clumps can be divided in autumn or spring.

ALTERNATIVES *R. f.* var. *deamii* ♔ is free flowering with very hairy stems. *R. hirta* cultivars (like 'Goldilocks' and 'Marmalade') are grown as annuals (see pages 100–1).

Sedum spectablile ♔
Ice plant
H and **S** 45cm/18in

This easy perennial has so much to offer. Plants die back for the winter and sprout again in spring, growing to form mound-like clumps of succulent grey-green leaves. In late summer and autumn, each stem terminates in a flattish head of small starry pink flowers which attract bees and butterflies.

POSITION In sun; sedums prefer a well-drained soil. Over-feeding can cause plants to grow too large and sappy, which makes the stems collapse when they come into bloom. Increase plants to create an edge to a border (see page 110).

Sedum spectabile **'Brilliant'**

MAINTENANCE Leave stems in place for the autumn and early winter, but remove when they become black and soggy. Plants are easy to divide in spring or autumn (see pages 34–5).

ALTERNATIVE *S.* 'Herbstfreude' ♔ ('Autumn Joy') is similar, but slightly larger and bears deep pink to copper-red flowers. I do not think this is as attractive to insects.

Verbena bonariensis
H 1.2–2m/4–6ft **S** 60cm/24in

Deservedly popular, this verbena produces plenty of stiff, upright, branching stems which end in small heads of purple flowers throughout summer and into autumn. There is little leaf to interfere with the display and the airy stems, scattered in drifts through beds and borders of informal perennials and grasses, attract many insects over a long period, including late butterflies.

POSITION In sun. Any well-drained soil will do, since this verbena is tough and able to thrive on poor sands; it copes with drought well. Prolonged periods of freezing temperatures, especially when soil is wet, can kill plants off.

MAINTENANCE. Cut back hard in spring and new growth will regenerate the plant. Short sideshoots will root easily during summer, four or five to a pot under polythene.

ALTERNATIVES Try *V. rigida* for a shorter display of purple flowers.

Verbena bonariensis

Brachyglottis (Dunedin Group) 'Sunshine' ♔

Senecio

H 1.4m/4ft S 1.5m/5ft

Tough silver-leaved evergreen shrub forming good mounds of foliage brightened in summer by masses of daisy-like yellow flowers. Leaves deserve scrutiny for their felting of white hairs and slightly scalloped margins, and are good for adding to cut flower arrangements.

POSITION In sun and well-drained soil; thrives on thin, sandy soils and also clays if not waterlogged in winter. Combines well with purple foliage and flowers. Its sweeping stems are ideal for creating structure towards the fronts of shrub borders.

MAINTENANCE Old, straggly plants can be cut back hard in spring and usually regenerate well.

ALTERNATIVE *B.* 'Drysdale' has delightfully crisp, wavy margins to its silvery leaves.

Buxus sempervirens

Buddleja davidii 'Dartmoor' ♔

Butterfly bush

H and S 3m/10ft

Long, tapering panicles of small, fragrant flowers that appear during summer act like magnets to many butterflies. In full sun, shrubs become alive with fluttering wings and jewel-like colours. This cultivar is exceptional in producing its rich, reddish-purple flowers in branching panicles. The leaves fall in winter.

POSITION Sun and fertile, well-drained soil ensure first-rate performances, but buddlejas will germinate in impossible-looking cracks and crevices in paving.

MAINTENANCE Pruning keeps size down and flower quality up. Cut most of last year's growth hard back in spring, leaving a few growth buds behind. This seems brutal, but the plant will flower the same year.

ALTERNATIVES *B. d.* 'Black Knight' ♔ bears dramatic, dark, purple-blue flowers. *B. d.* 'White Profusion' is a useful alternative to the pink/purple/blue colour range.

Buxus sempervirens ♔

Box

H and S to 5m/15ft

Usually clipped, box rarely reaches its unrestricted size. Its neat, dense evergreen foliage is ideal for hedges and topiary: box balls, pyramids and spirals that add strong structural elements to a garden. Box fares well in containers, making it usefully mobile. In sun or when cut, box has a characteristic, sharp aroma.

POSITION Well-drained but moist soil in part shade avoids drought stress resulting in ugly yellow leaves.

MAINTENANCE Trained shapes need clipping at least twice a year. Overgrown plants can be cut really hard back and will sprout again.

ALTERNATIVES For an ornamental evergreen, *B. s.* 'Marginata' bears yellow-edged leaves.

Caryopteris x clandonensis 'Heavenly Blue' ♔

H 90cm/3ft S 1.2m/4ft

An ideal shrub for a small garden, it produces a hazy effect, with toothed, aromatic grey-green foliage and many small deep blue flowers in late summer. Leaves fall in winter.

POSITION In sun and well-drained, but not necessarily rich, soil. A good drought-tolerant shrub which looks great with hardy fuchsias.

MAINTENANCE Keep plants compact and give them a longer life by pruning a good two-thirds back in early spring as buds break.

ALTERNATIVE *C. x c.* 'Worcester Gold' brings a splash of gold foliage throughout spring and summer.

Choisya ternata ♔

Mexican orange

H and S 1.8m/6ft

Strong performer making a rounded dense bush with a pleasing balance between evergreen foliage and white, fragrant orange-blossom-style flowers. These appear first in spring, with a second flush during summer and autumn.

POSITION In sun or part shade; it grows in most fertile soils as long as they do not hold water in winter.

MAINTENANCE Cut away old stems to improve shape. If frosts damage young plants, cut off damaged stems in late spring and the plant will regenerate.

ALTERNATIVE *C.* 'Aztec Pearl' ♔ has leaves composed of three to five linear leaflets that are more deeply cut and make jagged patterns.

Cornus alba 'Sibirica' ♔
Dogwood
H and S 1.8m/6ft

Grown for their colourful winter stems these superb plants tolerate wet soils, and give winter and sometimes year-round interest. In summer, when at their least interesting, their stems can be used as plant supports for floppy herbaceous perennials. This cultivar bears bright red winter stems and leaves that turn red in autumn.

POSITION For the best stem colours, in sun, though part shade is tolerated. Dogwood grows well in most soils from sands to clays.

MAINTENANCE For compact plants with the longest, brightest winter stems, cut almost all of the previous season's growth back to a ground-hugging framework in early spring.

ALTERNATIVES Choose *C. stolonifera* 'Flaviramea' ♔ for yellow-green stems, *C. sanguinea* 'Midwinter Fire' for orange, on a shorter plant. *C. alba* 'Spaethii' ♔ has glorious yellow-edged variegated summer foliage and red winter stems.

Corylus avellana 'Contorta'
Corkscrew hazel, twisted nut, Harry Lauder's walking stick
H and S 3m/10ft

A fabulous shrub, at its best in late winter and early spring when the sculptural, twisted stems are furnished with dangling, pale yellow catkins. Leafless, the cut stems are a favourite of flower arrangers.

POSITION In sun or part shade and good, well-drained soil; hazels thrive on chalk. Give this plant plenty of space in the garden, though it grows well restricted by containers.

MAINTENANCE Cut off any straight stems rising from below the graft union and thin out stems for a better appearance. Cut in late winter so as to use the stems in the house.

ALTERNATIVE *Salix babylonica* var. *pekinensis* 'Tortuosa' ♔, twisted willow, is fun to grow, though ultimately much larger unless pruned.

Cotinus coggygria 'Royal Purple' ♔
H and S 2.5m/8ft

Among the finest deciduous shrubs, this plant's dark reddish-purple large oval leaves glow beautifully with the light behind them. In autumn, they turn scarlet. The smoky-looking inflorescences are a complementary purple colour.

Cornus alba 'Sibirica' with *Epimedium perralderianum* ground cover

shrubs

POSITION In sun or light shade, but leaf colour is best in sun. Grows in any well-drained soil.

MAINTENANCE Smoke bushes mostly take care of themselves. If the plant looks tired, cut almost to ground level in early spring; it should send up vigorous stems with large leaves.

ALTERNATIVES All smoke bushes are pretty. Larger *C. coggygria* ♔ has smaller green leaves that colour well in autumn and show off its smoky flower and fruit panicles really well. *C. c.* 'Grace' ♔ has large plum-purple leaves turning red.

Cotoneaster simonsii ♔
H 2.5m/8ft S 1.8m/6ft

Bright but unpretentious upright shrub for a mixed border or as part of a hedge. Small, glossy, neat leaves turn bright red before autumn fall. Pink-tinged white flowers in summer are followed by a profusion of bright, orange-red fruits.

POSITION In sun; it is unfussy about soil and tolerates poor soils well.

MAINTENANCE Should plants need pruning because they are growing in a confined position, thin out the older, taller stems at any time, but preferably in late winter (see pages 74–5).

ALTERNATIVE *C. divaricatus* makes a more rounded deciduous shrub also offering autumn colour and a show of more subtle, dark red fruits.

Elaeagnus x ebbingei
H and S 2.5m/8ft

Mounds of metallic evergreen foliage are the key feature of this understated shrub. Leaf undersides are reflective silvery-white, surfaces are green and stems are covered with golden scales. In autumn, a sweet fragrance emanates from almost hidden, small creamy-white flowers.

POSITION In sun or part shade; it is unfussy about soils as long as they are not waterlogged. Place where winter sun makes the leaves glow.

MAINTENANCE Should shrubs outgrow their space, take out some of the longest stems and use them for flower arranging. If variegated alternatives start producing plain-leaved shoots, cut these out.

ALTERNATIVES *E.* x *e.* 'Gilt Edge' ♔ has brightly coloured leaves edged with gold (see pages 112–3). Those of *E. pungens* 'Maculata' ♔ are splashed with gold in the centre. The most silvery-leaved is deciduous *E.* 'Quicksilver'.

Erica x darleyensis 'White Perfection' ♔
Darley Dale heath, winter-flowering heather

H 40cm/16in S 75cm/30in

Valuable for their ground-cover habit and classy white flowers, these winter-flowering heathers thrive on most soils. Buds form during autumn, opening in late winter and spring. Peg stems of *Clematis* x *durandii* in between heathers for its summer blue flowers and prune it back every autumn.

POSITION In sun and in any well-drained soil.

MAINTENANCE Clip back straight after flowering to keep its compact, dense shape with masses of flowers.

ALTERNATIVES *E. carnea* 'Springwood White' ♔ is also good. There are many cultivars of *E. carnea* and *E.* x *darleyensis*, offering a variety of flower shades and leaf colours.

Euonymus alatus

Euonymus alatus ♔
Winged spindle

H 1.8m/6ft S 2.5m/8ft

This easy deciduous shrub is not as widely grown as it deserves, for it gives interest during every season. New leaves are a delicate pinkish colour, while in autumn the stops are out for a dazzling display of purple fruit with orange arils and bright red foliage. In winter corky wings decorate the sculptural four-angled stems and remaining fruits hang like ornaments.

POSITION In sun or light shade, but in autumn it needs sun to make it glow. Euonymus thrives in most soils and tolerates dry soils well.

MAINTENANCE In winter, tidy up the shrubs by removing weak stems or those causing congestion.

ALTERNATIVES *E. europaeus* 'Red Cascade' ♔, also deciduous, has red

Euonymus fortunei 'Emerald 'n' Gold'

autumn colour and larger red fruits with ornamental orange arils.

Euonymus fortunei 'Emerald 'n' Gold'

H 60cm/24in S 90cm/36in

A rather ubiquitous small shrub, but nevertheless valuable, as it provides a dense splash of golden evergreen ground cover. Its leaves have wide, bright gold margins and can turn pinkish during cold winters.

POSITION In sun or light shade; it suits most soils. Ideal for the fronts of borders, where it works well repeated. It is also invaluable for winter hanging baskets and containers.

MAINTENANCE Cut back portions which threaten to swamp other plants. Remove stems which layer or root themselves into the soil – they can be grown on separately.

Cuttings root easily.

ALTERNATIVES *E.f.* 'Emerald Gaiety' ♛ is similar, with leaves edged with cream, not gold. For *E.f.* 'Silver Queen' ♛, see page 150.

Fuchsia 'Riccartonii' ♛

Hardy fuchsia

H 1.8m/6ft S 1.2m/4ft

This is one of the toughest of the hardy fuchsias, producing single flowers in mid- to late summer. A classic dancing lady, with pink sepals or skirts and purple corollas. In mild regions, it grows tall and can be used as hedging. In colder areas where top growth is killed by frost, vigorous regrowth appears in spring.

POSITION In sun or part shade in fertile, well-drained soil.

MAINTENANCE Prune as hard as necessary in spring to remove frost-damaged growth and/or to win control over height. For the best display of flowers, apply a couple of doses of general-purpose liquid fertilizer in early summer.

ALTERNATIVES *F. magellanica* is delightfully wild-looking, with many slim, dainty red and purple flowers. Semi-double *F.* 'Alice Hoffman' has rose pink skirts and white corollas.

Hamamelis x *intermedia* 'Pallida' ♛

Witch hazel

H and S 4m/12ft

Flower buds formed towards the end of summer are carried through autumn to open during mid- to late winter. The eagerly awaited yellow flowers, fragrant and spidery, show up well against the tracery of leafless stems. Leaves turn a pleasant, buttery-yellow in autumn before falling.

POSITION In sun or part shade, in good, moist but well-drained soil. Avoid planting in shallow chalky soils. Try to set plants against a dark background so that their flowers will show up well.

MAINTENANCE Plants need watering during summer droughts if they are to set flower buds.

ALTERNATIVES *H.* x *i.* 'Jelena' ♛ bears flowers the colour of caramelized sugar. *H.* x *i.* 'Diane' ♛ bears dark red flowers and leaves turn brilliant red, yellow and orange in autumn.

Hamamelis x *intermedia* 'Pallida'

shrubs

145

Hydrangea 'Lanarth White'

Hebe 'Great Orme' ♔

H and S 1.2m/4ft

Hebes are valuable for their compact evergreen shapes and profuse flowering. Some are a little tender, but they are good seaside plants, as they benefit from the milder winters of some seaside areas, providing in return reliable salt-tolerant bushes. This hebe has elegant, tapering leaves and spikes of pink flowers from summer to autumn.

POSITION In sun or light shade in most soils; they tolerate poor soils.

MAINTENANCE Cut back overgrown, straggly plants hard in spring. There is a 90 per cent chance that they will survive. Cuttings root easily and are best taken in midsummer.

ALTERNATIVES There are many smaller, compact hebes, but of similar height is *H.* 'Midsummer Beauty' ♔, whose lilac flowers fade to white as they age.

Helianthemum 'Rhodanthe Carneum' ♔

Sun rose

H 30cm/12in S 75cm/30in

A low shrub making a carpet of silvery leaves during summer, studded by many, rounded, silky-petalled, pale pink flowers from late spring to midsummer.

POSITION In sun. Well-drained, neutral to alkaline soil suits sun roses well. They are useful for sunny banks, but are stunning in gardens mulched with shingle or gravel.

MAINTENANCE After flowering in midsummer, cut plants back to remove much of the flowered growth, but avoid cutting into old, hard wood. Bunch stems together and snip through with secateurs.

ALTERNATIVES *H.* 'Wisley White' has soft, creamy-white flowers, and *H.* 'Wisley Primrose' ♔ bears primrose yellow flowers with golden centres.

Hydrangea macrophylla 'Lanarth White' ♔

Lacecap hydrangea

H and S 1.5m/5ft

White-flowered hydrangeas are easy on the eye and none more so than this lacecap. Pink-tinged fertile flowers in the centre are surrounded by larger, showier, white sterile flowers in wide heads that open in mid- and late summer.

POSITION In sun or part shade. Soil should be humus-rich and moist, especially when plants are sited in full sun. Shelter from strong winds.

MAINTENANCE Remove dead flowerheads in spring, cutting to the first fat pair of buds down the stem. Restore overgrown plants by cutting out up to one third of the longer, older shoots to the base or lowest healthy sideshoot.

ALTERNATIVES *H. arborescens* 'Annabelle' ♔ bears large, white, rounded flowerheads of small sterile flowers on a larger plant.

Ilex aquifolium 'Ferox Aurea'

Hedgehog holly

H and S 1.2m/4ft

A spiny little male holly, whose gold-splashed leaves have prickles on their prickles. Being male, it sets no fruit, but it can pollinate female hollies. A good front-of-border evergreen, it grows slowly. It is mostly maintained below 1.5m/5ft, but will in fact grow a lot taller than this.

POSITION In sun or part shade. All hollies are tough, grow in virtually any soil and tolerate exposure to the elements well.

MAINTENANCE Trim back unwanted stems in spring as growth starts.

Ilex aquifolium 'Ferox Aurea'

ALTERNATIVES *I. a.* 'Ferox Argentea' bears cream-edged leaves. Holly-like evergreen *Osmanthus heterophyllus* 'Aureomarginatus' is variegated, less spiny and slow-growing.

Lavandula angustifolia 'Loddon Blue'
English lavender

H 60cm/24in S 90cm/36in

English lavender flowers in mid- to late summer, giving off its classic lavender fragrance and attracting lots of bees. This cultivar bears intensely purple-blue flower spikes.

POSITION In sun and well-drained soil; tolerates poor, dry soils. Ideal for low hedging and edgings as well as making good punctuation in borders (see pages 110–1).

MAINTENANCE Trim the plants over lightly after flowering, and give a more severe haircut in spring.

ALTERNATIVES The soft pink flower spikes of *L. a.* 'Loddon Anna' make a good contrast to the purples in mixed plantings. Great to look at, French lavender (*L. stoechas*) has characteristic purple bracts atop chunky flower spikes, but a perfume more akin to disinfectant.

Leycesteria formosa
Himalayan honeysuckle

H 1.8m/6ft S 1.5m/5ft

A tough but interesting deciduous shrub with year-round appeal. Stems are well clad with lush, heart-shaped leaves, joined by hanging 10cm/4in long spikes of purple-red bracts and white flowers from midsummer into autumn. Purple berries follow. Leaves fall to reveal attractive green, cane-like stems.

POSITION In sun or shade; it

Lavandula angustifolia 'Loddon Blue'

tolerates most soils and is a good seaside plant.

MAINTENANCE The youngest stems are the most attractive, so control each spring by cutting out the older stems that flowered last year.

ALTERNATIVES There are no comparable plants.

Lotus hirsutus
Hairy canary clover

H and S 90cm/3ft

A small rounded evergreen shrub of silvery, almost ghostly appearance, as its small leaves are covered with silky hairs. During summer and autumn, off-white pea-like flowers open, adding to the hazy, smoky effect. Handsome, shiny reddish-brown seed pods follow.

POSITION In sun, and must have well-drained soil to do well. It provides a great solution to a hot, dry bed where the soil is poor.

MAINTENANCE Prune straggly plants back hard in spring, but not into really old wood. Though not long-lived, they seed themselves well and root easily from cuttings in summer.

ALTERNATIVES There are no similar plants in the same group.

Magnolia stellata
Star magnolia

H and S 2.5–3m/8–10ft

One of the easiest magnolias to grow. In spring, silky buds open to large, starry white flowers up to 13cm/5in across, which show up against the tracery of branches. It settles down to being dense and leafy for the rest of the summer.

POSITION In sun or light shade. A well-drained, humus-rich soil is preferred. Tolerates chalk soils as long as they are not too dry.

MAINTENANCE Spread a deep mulch over the roots in spring.

ALTERNATIVES *M. s.* 'Waterlily' ♔ is spectacular, with flowers of up to thirty-two petals each. *M.* x *loebneri* 'Merrill' ♔ is a small tree bearing white, star-shaped flowers and tolerates chalk.

Mahonia aquifolium
Oregon grape

H 90cm/3ft S 1.2m/4ft

Though common, this tough North American evergreen should not be overlooked. In cold winters its holly-like leaves sometimes turn bright red. Dense heads of scented yellow flowers appear in early spring. Blue-black berries follow.

POSITION In sun or shade; it grows well in most soils and withstands competition from other plants amazingly well.

MAINTENANCE As older stems grow bare at the base, cut them low down when in bloom for the house. New shoots should grow from the cut.

ALTERNATIVES If space allows, grow tall architectural, winter-flowering mahonias like *M.* x *m.* 'Buckland' and *M.* x *media* 'Charity' ♔.

shrubs

Philadelphus 'Beauclerk'

Osmanthus delavayi ♀

H 1.8m/6ft   S 2.5m/8ft

At its peak in spring, this evergreen shrub bears small, toothed, shiny dark green leaves against which bunches of tubular, highly scented white flowers show up distinctly. It then fades into the background as a dark green stage set to show off performances of other plants.

POSITION In sun or part shade, in any good, well-drained soil out of cold winds, which can scorch the foliage. Can be used as hedging.

MAINTENANCE Maintain height and shape by pruning out unwanted stems either during (if you want them in the house) or just after flowering.

ALTERNATIVE *O.* x *burkwoodii* ♀ bears larger, mid-green leaves.

Philadelphus 'Beauclerk' ♀

Mock orange

H and S 2.5m/8ft

One of a tribe of popular, mostly tall, deciduous shrubs with single or double white scented flowers that bloom for a short period during early summer; this has large single flowers on slightly arching branches.

POSITION In sun or part shade; not fussy about soil, if not waterlogged.

MAINTENANCE Prune up to one third of the bush directly after flowering to keep plants to a manageable size and encourage a succession of new stems. Unpruned plants tend to become woody at the base with the flowers in the sky.

ALTERNATIVES Double-flowered *P.* 'Manteau d'Hermine' ♀ is 75cm/30in high but 1.5m/5ft in spread. *P.* 'Belle Etoile' ♀, 1.2m/4ft high, bears single white flowers blotched with purple in the centre.

Phormium 'Maori Sunrise'

New Zealand flax

H and S 90cm/3ft

This colourful, diminutive, usually slow-growing phormium is best placed where low shafts of evening sun back-light its sword-shaped, bronze-edged leaves, striped liberally with pink and apricot. Lovely with grasses and silvery-leaved plants.

POSITION In sun and well-drained soil; copes with poor sandy soils.

MAINTENANCE Remove dead leaves about twice a year.

ALTERNATIVES *P. tenax* ♀ forms an impressive clump 2.5m/8ft high and 1.8m/6ft in spread and flowers in summer. *P.* 'Sundowner' ♀ (H/S 1.5m/5ft) has bronze-hued leaves striped yellow and pink.

Phygelius capensis ♀

Cape figwort

H 1.2m/4ft   S 1.5m/5ft

An accommodating shrub which, if hit by severe frost, grows back from below ground. Suckers into a wide yet not invasive clump. Long panicles of tubular orange flowers appear in summer.

POSITION In sun and well-drained soil; tolerates droughts. Good for a border of reds, bronze and yellows.

MAINTENANCE Trim back dead stems after winter. Deadhead after first flush of flowers to encourage a second round. Mulch over the crowns in autumn in colder areas.

ALTERNATIVES Among the many attractive cultivars try *P.* x *rectus* 'Moonraker' for panicles of pale yellow flowers and *P.* 'Sensation' for magenta flowers that go well with silvers, purples and lilacs.

Pines mugo

Dwarf mountain pine

H 90cm/3ft   S 1.5m/5ft

This low-growing pine stays small for many years, especially on poor, sandy soils. Its branching, tree-like form and bright green needles make a good foil for other plants.

POSITION In sun and average, well-drained soil types.

MAINTENANCE Water in dry spells for the first eighteen months or so; it needs no maintenance thereafter.

ALTERNATIVES *P.m.* 'Mops' ♀ is compact and bushy but lacks the branch and needle structure of the species. *P. sylvestris* 'Beuvronensis' ♀ (H/S 90cm/3ft) is a dwarf form of the Scots pine. *P. flexilis* 'Firmament' is the dwarf form of the limber pine.

easy-care plants

Viburnum x *bodnantense* 'Dawn'

Viburnum tinus

Ribes sanguineum 'Brocklebankii' ♉
Flowering currant

H and S 1.2/4ft

Choice deciduous gold-leaved shrub that stays at 75–90cm/30–36in high for some time before reaching its full size. Useful for the front of a border. The foliage, acid-yellow at first, coincides with pink spring flowers in an exciting combination.
POSITION In sun or part shade, as harsh light can scorch the foliage. Suits any well-drained soil. Plant next to purple leaves and flowers.
MAINTENANCE Any pruning should take place straight after flowering, but is not normally necessary. Prune larger cultivars regularly.
ALTERNATIVE *R. alpinum* 'Aureum', 60cm/2ft high, gives a burst of yellow foliage and greenish yellow flowers.

Rosa 'Felicia' ♉

H 1.2m/4ft S 1.5m/5ft

Shrub roses are easy to care for and fit among other border plants. This bears glossy foliage and double flowers of soft, almost peachy pink, eventually revealing orange stamens, and a moderate fragrance. Flowers repeat throughout summer.
POSITION In sun or semi-shade and good, fertile soil for best results.
MAINTENANCE Light pruning in late winter or early spring to tidy plants.
ALTERNATIVES Of the many shrub roses, choose hybrid musks such as *Rosa* 'Penelope' ♉, with semi-double flowers of warm, peachy pink fading almost to white. Repeats throughout summer. Scent is rich and fruity.

Viburnum x *bodnantense* 'Dawn' ♉

H 2.7m/9ft S 1.8m/6ft

If this size sounds a little scary, a more modest 1.8m/6ft is possible by regular pruning. Clusters of small, pink, fragrant flowers open against dark winter twigs from late autumn to spring, in milder weather.
POSITION In sun or part shade, in any well-drained soil. Site where the shrub can be viewed easily during winter. Leaves are dull in summer, so front with some lively perennials.
MAINTENANCE Thin out older stems immediately after flowering.
ALTERNATIVES *V.* x *b.* 'Charles Lamont' ♉ has larger, imposing pink flowers. *V.* x *b.* 'Deben' ♉ has paler, almost white flowers.

Viburnum tinus 'Eve Price'
Laurustinus

H and S 3m/10ft

Many a gap is successfully filled with this evergreen, which is in bud or bloom for half the year, winter and spring. This cultivar is of dense habit and its flat, 12cm/4in-wide heads of small carmine buds open to pink-tinged, white flowers.
POSITION In sun or light shade in most soils. It grows tall, so site towards the backs of borders.
MAINTENANCE Cut back with care after flowering. Haphazard shearing can cause plants to refuse to flower.
ALTERNATIVE *V.t.* 'Lucidum' has slightly larger leaves and imposing heads of white flowers in spring.

shrubs

149

Abutilon x suntense
Hardy abutilon
H 4m/12ft S 2.5m/8ft

A high fence or wall is needed for this large deciduous shrub, but its stiff stems can support themselves beyond the top. Saucer-shaped flowers, produced in spring and early summer, are usually violet-blue, though the colour can vary.
POSITION In sun, and well-drained soil; tolerates poor, dry soils well. Plant with blue and white potato vines, which will use the abutilon as a climbing frame and provide later flowers.
MAINTENANCE Fix to horizontal wires or secure by tying stems to small nails. Shoots can be shortened after flowering.
ALTERNATIVES *A.* x *s.* 'Ralph Gould' bears slightly larger flowers of a reliable violet. For white, choose *A.* x *s.* 'Gorer's White'. *A. vitifolium* is hardy and similar, but plants can grow even larger.

Chaenomeles x speciosa
'Moerloosei' ♛
Apple blossom japonica, Japanese quince
H and S 1.5–2.5m/5–8ft

Japonicas are first-rate deciduous or semi-evergreens for bringing colour to cold, shaded walls. Clusters of cup-shaped flowers, in this case white and pink, open during late winter and early spring. Fruits that follow are used for jams and jellies.
POSITION Any aspect; tolerates most soils. The flexible stems are good for fan-training against a wall or fence.

MAINTENANCE Train in required stems. Shorten any not needed to five leaves after flowering.
ALTERNATIVES Plenty of other cultivars available with white, red, pink or salmon-coloured flowers.

Clematis 'Helsingbord'
Alpine clematis
H 3m/10ft S 1.5m/5ft

The spring-flowering clematis are easy to grow and rarely succumb to the dreaded clematis wilt which can affect large-flowered hybrids. This cultivar bears pointed purple-coloured sepals at the same time as bright new foliage develops.
POSITION In sun or shade, so suits any aspect. All clematis like a fertile, humus-rich soil. Plant them 10cm/4in deeper than root tops, which helps them grow back if damaged. Roots do best when shaded from hot sun. A good plant for a pergola.
MAINTENANCE The routine pruning of early-flowering species is not essential (see pages 42–3). Mulch over the roots in winter.
ALTERNATIVES *C. macropetala* and its cultivars perform well in spring. For later flowers, *C.* 'Etoile Violette' ♛ produces masses of 7cm/3in-wide purple flowers with yellow anthers. Late-flowering *C. viticella* and cultivars are equally easy-going.

Cytisus battandieri ♛
Moroccan broom, pineapple broom
H and S 4m/13ft

A delightful wall shrub which needs space to achieve its best, but can support itself above a wall or fence.

Clematis 'Helsingbord'

This semi-evergreen produces grey-green, silver-backed leaves which act as an excellent foil to candles of pineapple-scented, yellow, pea-like flowers opening in early summer.
POSITION An ideal solution for a poor, sun-baked position, and likes light, well-drained soil.
MAINTENANCE No routine pruning needed, but remove unwanted branches after flowering.
ALTERNATIVES *Piptanthus nepalensis* (evergreen laburnum) is a similar leguminous plant with blue-green leaves and unscented yellow flowers.

Euonymus fortunei 'Silver Queen' ♛
H 1.8m/6ft S 1.5m/5ft

A classy evergreen climber of great use and ornament. Mature leaves are elegant and tapering, being two shades of green in the centre, but edged irregularly with white. New growth is a warm yellow. Clings to its support with stem roots in a similar way to ivy.

POSITION In sun or shade, so suits any aspect. Grows in most soils. Use to clothe the base of walls, fences or pergolas where other climbers have shot upwards, leaving bare stems.

MAINTENANCE Trim back in spring if growth exceeds its bounds. Where growth comes away from the wall, it can be clipped with shears.

ALTERNATIVES No other is such an efficient climber.

Hedera helix 'Atropurpurea' ♈
Purple-leaved ivy
H 8m/25ft S 3.5m/12ft
Ivies are superb evergreen climbing plants and the shining purple-bronze leaves and narrow green veins of this cultivar are particularly handsome. Use it to introduce dark notes among light-coloured plants.

POSITION In sun or shade. Thrives in most soils, but prefers them slightly alkaline, moist and humus-rich.

MAINTENANCE Do not support young ivies artificially as they need a season to create a base framework from which new climbing stems will

Lonicera periclymenum 'Serotina'

grow. Check growth of mature plants in spring and autumn, cutting back as necessary to prevent invasion of windows and gutters.

ALTERNATIVES Good cultivars include large-leaved *H. colchica* 'Sulphur Heart' and bright yellow *H. helix* 'Buttercup'; marbled *H. h.* 'Luzii' looks great on tree trunks where it appreciates shelter.

Hydrangea anomala subsp. petiolaris ♈
Climbing hydrangea
H and S 6m/20ft or more
This large, self-clinging, deciduous climber is suitable for house walls, tall fences or to climb trees, where it is at its most magnificent. Summer flowers consist of heads, 25cm/10in across, of small fertile flowers surrounded by larger sterile florets.

POSITION Grows in sun or shade and is thus mostly used as a solution for shaded or part-shaded walls. Roots prefer to be cool and moist.

MAINTENANCE Trim back unwanted stems after flowering.

ALTERNATIVES Other useful climbers in the hydrangea family include *Schizophragma integrifolium* ♈.

Jasminum nudiflorum ♈
Winter jasmine
H and S 1.2–3m/4–10ft
This, one of the commonest garden plants, is virtually indispensable for its reliable and cheerful profusion of yellow flowers along bare stems in winter, lasting for a long period. Plants are tough and durable.

POSITION In sun or shade in any well-drained soil. Grow with *Cotoneaster horizontalis* for a bright late-autumn show of berries, red

Jasminum nudiflorum

foliage and yellow flowers. Also looks good with ivy.

MAINTENANCE After flowering, fix stems to their framework, then shorten flowered, unwanted sideshoots by cutting back to short spurs. Continue to train as growth progresses during summer, but avoid further pruning.

ALTERNATIVES No other jasmine is as tough and reliable. *J. officinale* ♈ has perfumed white flowers in summer.

Lonicera periclymenum 'Serotina'
Honeysuckle, woodbine
H 4.5m/15ft S 2.2m/7ft
Honeysuckles are twining, self-clinging climbers well-suited to arches, pergolas and trellis, where they associate well with climbing roses. Most produce attractive berries after the flowers. This 'late Dutch' honeysuckle has late, richly coloured, white and pink flowers.

POSITION In sun or part shade. It suits all aspects and grows well in all soils, but a moist, fertile but well-drained soil gives the best results.

MAINTENANCE Prune back after flowering.

ALTERNATIVES *L. p.* 'Belgica' ♔, 'early Dutch', has white, yellow and pink flowers in early summer. The white, fragrant flowers of *L. p.* 'Graham Thomas' ♔ turn yellow as they age over a long period in summer. *L. x americana* ♔ and *L. caprifolium* ♔, Italian honeysuckle, are also pretty and fragrant and worth trying.

Parthenocissus tricuspidata ♔
Boston ivy
H and S 15m/50ft or more

In general, people either love to cover their houses with plants or they dislike the growth, worry about their walls and moan about the proximity of insects, spiders and birds. This plant with attractive three-lobed leaves clings by means of tendrils bearing little suckers. Leaves turn brilliant scarlet and purple in autumn, falling to leave a tracery of stems and dark blue berries.

POSITION In sun or shade; it grows in any well-drained soil.

MAINTENANCE The stems, although self-clinging, have a habit of coming away from walls if not secured here and there to masonry nails. Curb the growth of established plants twice a year to prevent stems from entering lofts and swamping roofs.

ALTERNATIVE *P. quinquefolia* ♔ bears attractive palmate leaves which also turn brilliant colours before falling.

Passiflora caerulea ♔
Blue passion flower
H and S 1.2–2.7m/4–9ft

This is the most reliable of the passion flowers, capable of flowering from summer to autumn every year in most areas. Petals (strictly tepals) are white and filaments are banded purple, white and blue. Orange fruits follow, which though edible, are not very palatable. Hard winters may kill the upper parts back, but growth will usually return from the base or below ground.

POSITION In sun or light shade; plants perform best in poor, well-drained soil. Being effective tendril climbers, they are ideal for clothing wire fences.

MAINTENANCE Large plants can be pruned back in spring before growth starts, to prevent them from outgrowing their bounds.

ALTERNATIVES Paler *P. c.* 'Constance Elliot' ♔ is almost white. *P. incarnata* (Maypops) and *P.* 'Incense' perform less well in cool summers.

Pyracantha 'Teton'
Firethorn
H and S 3m/10ft

Common they may be, but a well-trained pyracantha growing against a wall is a handsome sight. Shiny evergreen foliage, heads of small

Pyracantha 'Teton'

white flowers in late spring and bright orange berries in autumn give a first-class performance.

POSITION In sun or shade. A fertile, well-drained soil gives the best results and strongest plants.

MAINTENANCE Tie stems in as they grow. Thereafter, prune back carefully in early summer, usually cutting off most of the sideshoots to leave spurs bearing two or three leaves. Take care not to cut off the clusters of developing berries.

ALTERNATIVES 'Orange Glow' ♔,

Parthenocissus tricuspidata

gold 'Soleil d'Or' and red 'Mohave' are just three of many cultivars offering these bright berry colours.

Rhamnus alaternus 'Argenteovariegata' ♈
Variegated Italian buckthorn
H 1.2–5m/4–15ft S 2m/8ft

A first-rate evergreen maintained as a small shrub if clipped regularly, but plants will romp up high fences or walls to give a dense covering. Small narrow grey-green leaves are edged with white. Small yellowish flower clusters appear in late spring.
POSITION A sun-drenched wall is best. It grows in any well-drained soil and tolerates poor, dry soils.
ALTERNATIVES No other rhamnus performs the same role. *Pittosporum tenuifolium* and its cultivars exhibit similar neatness of foliage but are less dense and do not respond so well to clipping.

Rosa 'Climbing Etoile de Hollande' ♈
H 5m/15ft S 3m/10ft

There are many climbing roses, old and modern, from which to choose.

Rosa 'Etoile de Hollande'

This vigorous, rather stiff-stemmed rose bears large, fragrant double, deep red flowers throghout summer.
POSITION In sun or light shade. In common with all roses, a rich, fertile soil is preferred. However climbers, more than bush roses, can perform well on poorer, drier soils. It is ideal for pergolas and arches.
MAINTENANCE Tie in the main framework of stems. Thereafter, prune back as necessary, shortening the long sideshoots, every late winter or early spring. Water during droughts, especially next to walls.
ALTERNATIVES Noisette *R.* 'Madame Alfred Carrière' ♈ produces double, fragrant white flowers flushed with pink from late spring to autumn. 'New Dawn' is a pretty pink and 'Alchymist' a rich apricot colour.

Solanum crispum 'Glasnevin' ♈
Chilean potato vine
H and S 3m/10ft

A vigorous twining semi-evergreen climber bearing clusters of mauve-purple potato-like flowers with gold stamens from mid- to late summer.
POSITION In sun. It grows in most well-drained soils, and does well in poor, dry soils. It looks great on its own or as a climbing companion for other plants. Try it with the hardy abutilons, as solanum starts to bloom just as their last flowers fade.
MAINTENANCE Encourage a framework of stems to climb where needed. Thereafter, invasive stems can be pruned back immediately after flowering or in spring just as growth starts.
ALTERNATIVES *S. laxum* 'Album' is the slightly later, white-flowered potato vine.

Wisteria sinensis

Wisteria sinensis ♈
Chinese wisteria
H and S 3.5–6m/12–20ft

The deciduous queen of climbers is entirely desirable, though not low maintenance. Racemes of scented, pea-like flowers open in early summer and sometimes again in late summer. Buy in bloom to prove that the plant can flower and to tell which one it is.
POSITION In sun or part shade. It likes good, moist, well-drained soil.
MAINTENANCE Plants need careful training in their early years to create a framework. Tie stems in as they grow but shorten by one third during winter (see pages 44–5). Plants climbing trees need no pruning.
ALTERNATIVES Plant *W.s.* 'Alba' ♈ for white flowers. For longer racemes, plant *W. floribunda* (Japanese wisteria).

climbers and wall shrubs

Note: While establishing young plants, always water the roots during the first two summers.

Acer pensylvanicum 'Erythrocladum' ♈

Moosewood

H and S 9m/30ft

White-striped green bark and yellow autumn leaf tints of the species are overshadowed by this stunning cultivar, with its radiant pink new shoots. It is painfully slow-growing and so suited to smaller gardens.

POSITION In sun or part shade, and fertile, moist but well-drained soil.

MAINTENANCE Check tree ties often. Keep weeds away from the trunk.

ALTERNATIVE *A. conspicuum* 'Phoenix' has similar coloured stems and is easier to grow. *A. grosseri* var. *hersii* ♈, the Chinese snake bark, has green and white older stems, and younger ones pinkish-red, snaked with white.

Acer pensylvanicum 'Erythrocladum'

Amelanchier lamarckii ♈

Snowy mespilus, juneberry

H 10m/36ft S 12m/40ft

Good, all-year interest is available from this North American tree which takes some while to reach its fullest possible height. For a smaller, shrubbier effect, choose multi-stemmed plants. Dainty white spring blossom opens at the same time as the soft, bronze, oval leaves that turn green as they mature. Dark, edible berries may follow. Autumn colour is orange-red.

POSITION In sun or light shade. It tolerates most soils as long as they are not alkaline (chalky). Prefers a fertile, moist, yet well-drained soil.

MAINTENANCE In late winter, thin congested stems to maintain a lovely shape. Keep the base weed-free.

ALTERNATIVES *A. laevis* is similar, from which *A. × grandiflora* 'Ballerina' ♈ is a good hybrid – a floriferous small tree (H 6m/20ft S 8m/25ft).

Betula ermanii

Erman's birch

H 20m/70ft S 12m/40ft

There are many fine birches which, though they grow tall, tend to be slender and produce a light, airy effect casting little dense shade. This has cream-coloured bark tinged with orange-pink and bears dainty leaves, turning yellow in autumn.

POSITION In sun or dappled shade. It grows well in all well-drained soils, being particularly good at tolerating poor, dry soils.

MAINTENANCE Gradually clear the

Amelanchier lamarckii

main stem by removing sideshoots as plants grow. Keep weeds and grass away from the trunk.

ALTERNATIVES The silver birch (*B. pendula*) is lovely and looks great in a group. Its weeping form, *B. p.* 'Youngii' ♈, is much shorter, but dome-shaped. *B. utilis* var. *jaquemontii* has a white trunk.

Crataegus laevigata 'Paul's Scarlet'

May, hawthorn

H and S 65m/20ft

A small, very hardy, thorny, dense tree well furnished with small leaves and covered by heads of dark pink, double flowers in late spring. It provides good shelter for birds.

easy-care plants

POSITION In sun or part shade. It grows in any well-drained soil and can tolerate exposure to wind. It is also ideal as a lawn specimen tree.
MAINTENANCE For a good 'tree-like' shape, buy a trained standard. Prune to thin out stems in the developing head during winter if necessary.
ALTERNATIVES *C. l.* 'Plena' bears double white flowers turning pink with age. For fruits, grow semi-evergreen *C.* x *lavallei* 'Carrierei' ♕ or *C. pedicellata,* both of which bear white flowers, show orange-red autumn colour and red fruits.

Cupressus sempervirens 'Totem Pole'

Italian cypress

H 6m/20ft S 90m/3ft

For bringing Mediterranean style to a garden, these pencil-thin cypresses can hardly be bettered as statement plants. This one is particularly good at growing up but not out. Scale-like leaves are deep green.
POSITION In sun. Avoid exposed, windy sites. It grows well in any well-drained soil and is particularly good for colonizing poor, dry soils.
MAINTENANCE Make sure other plants do not shade or swamp growth, which may then become damaged and will not regrow.
ALTERNATIVES *C. s.* 'Swane's Gold' ♕ is similarly narrow, but furnished with yellow-green leaves.

Pyrus communis 'Doyenné du Comice'

Pear tree

H and S 3.7–6m/12–20ft

Pear trees are longer-lived than apples and wreath the garden in pretty white blossom in spring. The choice of cultivar is a matter for personal taste but this one is a universal favourite.
POSITION In sun, with shelter from wind; avoid frost pockets. A fertile, well-drained soil is ideal.
MAINTENANCE Pear trees can be as low or high maintenance as you want. They are pruned in the same way as apple trees (see pages 38–9). A pollinator, a tree from the same group, must be near by.
ALTERNATIVES Apple trees flower after pears and offer more flexibility of height. MM106 is semi-dwarfing, resulting in a robust small tree. Varieties grafted on to M26 yield smaller trees 2.5–4m/8–12ft high. There are plenty of cultivars, but research will lead you to those most suited to your area.

Pyrus salicifolia 'Pendula' ♕

Weeping silver pear

H 4–5m/12–15ft S 4m/12ft

Deciduous tree of graceful weeping habit, with narrow, silvery, felted leaves sweeping to the ground. Creamy flowers open in spring.
POSITION In sun, in well-drained soil. Use in borders where the silvery foliage makes a good backdrop for greens, bronzes and blues.
MAINTENANCE Under trees in lawns, it is best to keep a circle of bare soil around it. Plant with spring bulbs.
ALTERNATIVE *Elaeagnus* 'Quicksilver' gives a similar silvery backdrop.

Sorbus cashmiriana ♕

Kashmir rowan

H 6m/20ft S 5.5m/18ft

A light-bodied, deciduous tree of dainty, dark green leaflets and heads of soft pink flowers in spring. Bears generous clusters of long-lasting berries, pink-tinged clearing to almost porcelain white by the time the leaves fall. Skeletal trees and white berries appear almost surreal.
POSITION In sun or dappled shade. Soil should be moist, yet well-drained, since trees tend to frizzle up on dry, impoverished soils. Avoid alkaline soils and add leaf mould.
MAINTENANCE None required.
ALTERNATIVES *S. aucuparia,* the orange-berried rowan or mountain ash, is lovely, as is *S. koehneana* ♕, a smaller, white-berried type. *S. vilmorinii* ♕, also small, is dainty and bears pink berries.

Pyrus communis 'Doyenné du Comice'

the living garden

the garden environment 158

the soil and its content 160

compost-making 162

weeds and the half-hour gardener 164

**pests, diseases and the
half-hour gardener** 166

0

10

15

20

25

30

the garden environment

MY LOVE OF GARDENING GREW IN TANDEM with a fascination for the whole outdoor world. For instance, I quickly learned to appreciate flowers like roses, with their sensuous petals and beguiling scents, but I was equally enthralled by the idea of the rose bush as a kind of apartment block for the myriad life forms of the garden. Close-up, I watched ants hurrying up and down stems to shepherd their 'flocks' of aphids. Clustered around the aphid colonies were predatory ladybirds and their strange lizard-like larvae. Greenfly, larger flies

These apple trees in my garden provide blossom and fruit, but like the meadow beneath them are also popular with a wide range of birds and insects.

and even wasps were caught in the webs of orb spiders and if I stood back, birds like blue tits would arrive to eat the pests that were eating the roses.

In a healthy garden every turn of the fork or spade is a revelation. Wolf spiders dart over the surface of the soil, sometimes carrying their spiderlings on their backs. Violet ground beetles scuttle over clods of earth, where they find their chief prey: slugs. Worms contract into their tunnels, interrupted from their sterling work as aerators of the soil, and when the gardener retreats, robins swoop down to pick up soil dwellers left on the surface. Wireworms, pupae such as leatherjackets and worms are all eagerly scooped up and eaten.

Rosebuds act as magnets for aphids, but birds and other predators eventually clear them away. Or you can just squash them between finger and thumb.

Pesticides or predators?

My enjoyment of a garden is bound up in the satisfaction of watching nature taking place before my eyes. Why intervene with pesticides on a large scale, or any scale at all, when you can see the job being done for you? Kill pests and you are taking away somebody's food. You may even be killing pest predators and parasites which would have not only done the job for you, but continued to do it all season long. For me, there is no joy in a sterile garden, however perfect its flowers and produce.

The advantages gained by the time-pressed gardener willing to minimize the use of pesticides are obvious. Think of all the time it would take to buy, mix and spray on a regular basis! My advice is to keep a keen eye on the garden and intervene only when a treasured plant is at risk, in which case treat it in isolation. The only pesticide I applied to my garden over a five-year period was when my lovely Pinsapo fir (*Abies pinsapo*) was thick with conifer aphids and there were no predators in sight. One quick blast with an aerosol containing the specific aphicide Pirimicarb and they all died and fell off. My more normal reaction to weak or pest- and disease-prone plants is to whip them out and replace then with more robust alternatives. This goes for lupins, which can succumb to those revoltingly large lupin aphids, and rose cultivars that suffer, year after year, with mildew and black spot.

Encourage pest devourers

Birds are great for the garden, because they eat so many pests. Sadly, some, like song thrushes, are in decline. On a quiet day, these delightful birds reveal themselves by a tapping sound like water dripping on stone. This is the sound of a hapless snail being thrashed against a stone (the thrush often uses the same favourite stone repeatedly) until its shell breaks and the thrush can eat it. To ensure the health of my garden birds, I feed them year round with good-quality bird food, which attracts them, keeps them healthy yet does not stop their natural foraging. Although gardeners can go out of their way to include berried plants and thicket-like shrubs to provide food, roosting and nesting sites for birds, flat-topped flowers to attract hoverflies and the food and nectar plants of moths and butterflies, most well-planted gardens will contain elements of these anyway. By avoiding excessive use of pesticides and fertilizers, not disturbing hedges and thickets during the nesting season, nourishing the soil with well-rotted compost and generally taking a back seat, you can watch the garden taking care of itself.

the living garden

159

the soil and its content

COMPOSED OF SMALL MINERAL PARTICLES, decayed organic matter, air and water, soil is the thin layer which, more or less, covers the land, offering all that plants need to sustain themselves. Good, fertile soil consists of half solids (mostly mineral, with some organic matter), and half pore spaces between the solids. In its most fertile state, half of these pores will be filled by air and half by water.

For good growth, plants need to obtain from the soil the three major elements: nitrogen, phosphorus and potassium. These should be present anyway, but can also be added by applying fertilizers (always listed on the bottle or packet in the same order, often as N:P:K). By and large, nitrogen promotes leafy growth, phosphates promote healthy root systems and potassium encourages flowers and fruit to set. But this is not the end of the story, because plants must also have calcium, magnesium, sulphur and a range of micronutrients or trace elements that includes iron, manganese, copper, zinc, boron, molybdenum, chlorine and cobalt. These are present in most soils and plants will generally grow strongly without their gardeners having to worry about them. However, on sandy, peaty or very alkaline soils, there can be nutrient deficiencies which affect some plants. Iron deficiency is one; that is why the leaves of rhododendrons turn a sickly yellow when they are grown on chalky soils. Magnesium and calcium, carried by most limestones, can be missing in acid soils.

Soil environment and condition

Our soil is also home to a huge range of life forms, including countless microorganisms which break down the organic matter that arrives on the soil as dead plant and animal matter. Humus, the well-rotted result, is an excellent soil conditioner, providing sulphur, phosphorus and nitrogen as well as retaining water and the nutrients dissolved within it.

Understanding soil composition is the key to offering plants what they need in order to grow. As gardeners, we may have little control over the soil type of our plot, but we can improve matters by digging in soil conditioner (see pages 22–3) at least to alleviate some of the imperfections. Whether soil is sand or clay, acid or alkaline, there will always be plenty of plants that will thrive in it. Many plants are surprisingly unfussy; others can be matched with soil type (see individual entries in the directory on pages 122–55).

Know your soil type

A good approach to finding out what kind of soil you have is to look at the soil's texture. Grab a handful of moist soil, squeeze it together and see what it does. The particles of a sandy soil might cling together intially, but try throwing the ball of soil up and down gently and it soon disintegrates. Rub some between your fingers and feel the grains of sand rasping against your skin. Unfortunately, water and nutrients slip through sand like the grains through your fingers, making it a hostile soil for some plants. The opposite is a heavy clay soil, which, being made up of minute particles, sticks together in a solid lump and will not disintegrate. This may be infuriating in the garden when it sets into a solid lump, and can be bad for plants because there is less air in the soil. But water and nutrients are held by the surfaces of these minute clay particles, making it potentially very fertile. The best soil of all is loam, which is a mixture of clay with just the right amount of sand and organic matter, combining nutrient and water-holding properties with good, workable texture and air for plants' roots.

A gardener in posession of a clay or sandy soil will gradually win by adding as much organic matter (well-rotted garden compost and manure) as possible. In the case of clay soil, add sharp sand or small-grade pea shingle as well to open the soil up. Do not add fine sand, as the particle size is too small and it will not be beneficial.

Keep your soil in good heart, and strong healthy plants will follow naturally.

Most plants thrive well on clay, especially roses. Heavy clays that become waterlogged during winter are not good for plants that come from dry, impoverished soils and the warm climates of some Mediterranean countries, or from high altitudes in South America and from a wide range of habitats in Australia and New Zealand. These plants (such as cistus, cytisus, lavenders, grevilleas, thymes, origanums, pittosporums, zauschnerias) give themselves away by bearing small, sometimes crinkly, hairy, shiny or silvery foliage which is adapted to lessen moisture loss. In clay they will be apt to rot unless drainage is improved. All thrive on dry, poor, sandy soils as they benefit from the free drainage and are adapted to growing where nutrients and water are low.

Soil acidity and alkalinity

Acidity and alkalinity content is measured as a pH value. A low pH such as 3 indicates extremely acid soil, while 11 is extremely alkaline; 7 is neutral.

When chalky lumps appear in soils, they give it away as alkaline, with a high pH number. But many soils keep their pH secrets to themselves and the only way to discover them is to carry out a soil test. Kits are usually cheap and a good investment against potential costly disasters such as buying acid-loving rhododendrons, pieris and camellias for alkaline soils on which they will not thrive. An initial, less sophisticated method is to look over the garden fence. If rhododendrons are growing well in neighbouring gardens, they probably will in yours, as your soil is likely to be the same. But watch out for canny gardeners who have created raised beds of acid soil by adding peat (though for environmental reasons few gardeners now use peat as a soil acidifier), leaf mould and pine needle mould.

Acidity and alkalinity content plays funny games with soil nutrients, making them either less available or too concentrated. In general, high pH (alkalinity) tends to restrict the availability of iron, manganese, phosphorus and zinc, whereas acid soils can be low in nutrients generally because the rate of decomposition slows down. A lot of gardeners react to alkaline or chalky soils with horror, yet there is no shortage of plants they can grow. Gardeners on acid soils tend not to moan, especially if they like woodland plants, but if they want to grow good cabbages, they will have to dress their vegetable plots with crushed limestone. Add lime sparingly along with plenty of organic matter, following instructions carefully.

THROUGHOUT THIS BOOK, I HAVE STRESSED the importance of conditioning the soil whenever digging, mulching and planting, by adding humus, which provides and holds nutrients and helps hold water. So where does all this marvellous, well-rotted material come from? Although horse manure and other soil conditioners can be brought in to the garden, they can cost money, time or both and can sometimes be disappointing in quality. The best source is one's own compost, home-made from vegetable waste generated by the garden and kitchen. To transform this material into a lovely dark brown crumbly soil conditioner which has cost nothing and can be returned to the soil, whence much of it came, is eminently satisfying.

There are good reasons for bothering to rot down this vegetable waste, rather than using it unrotted, as for instance in spreading lawn clippings between plants. First, it is much easier to deal with when reduced to crumbly particles and more importantly, unrotted material added straight to soil will rob it of nitrogen instead of enriching it, at least in the short term. This is because the bacteria which rot the waste down use nitrogen in the process, which they take from the soil. Eventually, when decomposition is completed, the bacteria die off, releasing nitrogen back to the soil, but until then plants are denied nitrogen, which can affect their health.

Bins, barrels or heaps?

Composting is simple, but there are potential pitfalls. The first challenge lies in deciding what to make the compost in. Beautifully constructed, slatted wooden bins for larger gardens or neat little plastic barrels for smaller ones hidden behind a shrub or fence would be the most attractive and serviceable. If you lack the time or money to construct or buy these, a heap will do just as well and is the method which has served my family for at least the last three generations. Grandad was a compost heaper, Father heaped and yes, I heap too.

Until recently (when I gardened in a drier climate, on better-drained soil) I always built my heaps directly on to the soil, which is good because the bacteria, worms, funghi and other soil life in charge of decomposition simply make their way up into the heap. Where rainfall is high and the soil at all waterlogged, build a base layer of twiggy sticks first, so that air can circulate.

Compost ingredients

Just as we need a varied diet, so does the compost heap. Place a waste bin with a lid near the kitchen door and use this to collect vegetable and fruit peelings. I would not add cooked food or bread, because these could attract rodents and foxes. Grass clippings, soft plant material and weeds can be gathered from the garden. Do not use perennial weeds or those which are seeding. Finely shredded stems, wood ash, pets' bedding (hay or straw and torn-up newspaper), seaweed, the contents of the vacuum cleaner bag and fallen leaves are all prime ingredients. It is important to add the different ingredients to the heap or container in loose, thin layers, approximately 5cm/2in deep, because too much of one thing will cause problems. Grass clippings, for instance, turn wet and slimy if in too dense a layer. A variety of textures means that air can move in the heap. If you have too much of one ingredient, pile it separately and throw it in gradually, alternating it with other ingredients.

the living garden

Every so often, it is a good idea to shovel on a thin layer of soil, which provides a boost of microorganisms. This often happens naturally, when you add weeds with soil on their roots. Ideally, after every 30cm/12in of added height, extra nitrogen should be added to fuel up the bacteria. Any kind of manure, nitrogen-rich fertilizer or proprietary compost activators will do this job and make for a hot, efficient heap. I rely on small but regular additions of pet droppings.

It is good, though not essential, to turn a compost heap occasionally, which mixes the rotting ingredients even more thoroughly and involves more air. In doing so, you should see lots of pink brandling worms, centipedes and wood lice. If these are working well and multiplying, it is likely that the invisible decomposers are thriving too. I don't have time to turn my heap, but I have evolved a method of piling the unrotted stuff all on to one side of the heap, to get at the crumbly rotted

Making compost is hugely satisfying. It is amazing to think that all the ingredients eventually reduce into a dark, crumbly material.

matter underneath. When I've dug this out, I put all the unrotted matter into the hole left and can then gain access to the remaining well-rotted compost. Then I level off the pile and carry on heaping. From start to finish I reckon that compost takes a year to rot this way, but I could take from the heap twice a year if I wanted. If you are using bins, a set of three allows for one in a finished state ready for use, one halfway there and the third filling with new waste.

Compost should be moist and may need watering during dry weather, but it can also become too wet, claggy and cold. To conserve moisture, cover dry heaps with something like old carpets and protect wet heaps with a waterproof covering such as polythene.

the living garden

weeds and the half-hour gardener

WEEDS ARE A FASCINATING GROUP OF PLANTS which inevitably introduce a note of philosophy into gardening. After all, what are weeds but unwanted plants – that is, plants growing in the wrong places? Under this definition, some cultivated plants can be weeds and so-called weeds can be desirable 'wild' flowers.

However, it is difficult to imagine anyone wanting to cultivate the worst perennial weeds on purpose. These include ground elder (*Aegopodium podagraria*), which dies back in winter, but remains alive as a mass of white, spaghetti-like roots growing thickly just under the soil surface, and also penetrating deeply. The leaves look superficially like those of a strawberry plant and come bounding up out of the soil as soon as spring arrives. Umbels of white flowers appear on unweeded plants, proclaiming kinship with the carrot and cow parsley family. Small infestations can be weeded by hand, but every tiny section of root left behind will sprout a new plant, so it is essential to keep returning to weed out regrowths. The application of a glyphosate-based weedkiller works well, since the chemicals are taken up by healthy, strong-growing foliage and taken down to the roots, killing both. But even this is unlikely to effect complete eradication in just one application. My own preference is for hand weeding, not least because I find drawing those roots through the soil quite mesmerizing.

Dealing with an infestation

Where a whole garden is infested with perennial weeds growing in and around the roots of desirable plants, the efficiency of both hand weeding and weedkiller is limited. The former will disturb the plants, whose roots, in any case, will be inextricably tangled with those of the weed. Glyphosate, if applied indiscriminately, will kill the good plants along with the bad. In the short term I would suggest putting up with a weed such as ground elder, but planting strong-growing perennials that make lots of spreading leafy growth (such as bergenia, Japanese anemone, *Geranium palmatum*), which will gradually swamp the weed or at least prevent it from making much headway. It will not go away, but will be far less obvious. At the same time, plant to clean the garden up area by area by digging out all the plants, controlling the weed then replanting. Much the same tactic can be applied to other nasty perennial weeds such as couch grass and *Calystegia* (bindweed or bellbine).

The two worst horrors

There are two weeds whose toughness and ineradicability put them in a league all of their own. One is Japanese knotweed (*Persicaria japonica*), for which we have the Victorians to thank. They thought it handsome with its cane-like stems reaching 1.8m/6ft, heart-shaped leaves and foamings of small creamy-white flowers. We now see it for what it is: a thicket-forming, deep-rooting menace. Digging this one out is far more difficult than coaxing ground elder from the soil. Even smothering is difficult, because of the sheer strength of its thrusting spring growth. I have seen Japanese knotweed shoots push easily through tarmac and concrete.

Successive applications of glyphosate-based weedkiller is probably the best approach. This is more readily absorbed if the leaves are crushed and broken slightly first. This tactic also works on field horsetail (*Equisetum arvense*), my second nomination for worst perennial weed. These primitive-looking plants are descended from species which have changed little in the last fifty million or so years. They produce silica deposits on their stems and leaves, giving them a strange, sandpaper-like quality – indeed they have a history of being used as natural pan-scourers. There are records of their roots having penetrated 10m/30ft below the ground.

Weeding tactics

Annual weeds may be an irritation, but are far easier to weed out than their perennial counterparts. Hoeing is a quick way of weeding between plants, the sharp blade slicing the weeds from their roots as well as cutting the roots from the soil. Hoe in dry weather so that the weeds will frizzle up on the soil surface. But a well-planted garden will take on a life of its own, with hellebores, honesty, sweet rocket, poppies and heartsease pansies sending their own seedlings up all over the place. The time-pressed gardener would be a fool not to capitalize on these easy and free gap-fillers, which means that hoeing is out. Instead, a more selective weeding tactic is needed. Using a border or hand fork and keeping your eyes to the ground, remove weeds and thin out seedlings, all in the same manoeuvre.

Annual weed leaves such as chickweed, speedwell, groundsel and fat hen, and the tops of some perennials (nettles and willow herb are easily separated from their roots), can be added to the compost heap. But bag up perennial weeds and dispose of them, along with the seeding heads of annual weeds because these can cause a lot of extra work if not removed from the garden.

Perennial weeds such as this ground elder should be allowed nowhere near the compost heap, for fear of their roots persisting and being recycled into the garden when the compost is used as mulch or conditioner.

THIS SECTION COVERS SOME OF THE MOST COMMON plant problems such as non-flowering bulbs and shrubs, nutrition deficiencies, unhealthy leaves, and pests such as insects and aphids. The healthiest attitude towards the more negative side of gardening is to view these potential problems with curiosity and an open mind.

Why plants refuse to flower

Young shrubs bought in bloom cause concern when they fail to flower in successive years. Sometimes, when planted out and suddenly finding themselves free of their containers, they invest all their energy into root and stem growth and will flower when ready. Examples include magnolias, abelia and philadelphus (mock orange).

Insufficient light can prevent mature shrubs from flowering, as can bad pruning. Many spring- and early summer-flowering shrubs produce their flower buds on stems that grew during the previous season. If these are cut off during autumn or winter, there will be no flowers. Either prune at the correct time (usually directly after flowering) or if unsure, follow the general guidelines for pruning on page 74–5.

Wisterias can infuriate their owners by not producing flowers for twelve, fifteen or even twenty years. They need careful siting, pruning and training (see pages 44–5), and lack of these may be the cause of the problem, but long-term failure can often be blamed on bad seed-raised plants with no pedigree. By buying a wisteria when it is in bloom, not only do you have living proof of its flowering ability, but you can also check that it is the type you want.

Smaller plants and bulbs that refuse to flower may need a boost of high-potash fertilizer (a tomato-type fertilizer).

Bulbs, particularly daffodils, sometimes come up blind, for a variety of reasons. It is important to allow their leaves to remain (unknotted) for a minimum of six weeks after flowering, to fuel the bulbs for the following year (some plant food will help, especially on poor soils). Excessively dry summers can lead to poor results. Congestion is a common problem, especially on clay soil. Bulbs which have multiplied underground have no room to expand and become crammed together. If this is the case, lift, divide and replant singly while the bulbs are in growth.

Causes of blemished leaves

There is a whole legion of leaf-spotting fungi, many specific to one type of plant, that cause splodges and spots on foliage. In most cases, they are not worth worrying about and the most action one might want to take is to clear up and dispose of fallen leaves to minimize future infections. The fungi can, to an extent, be controlled by spraying with relevant fungicides, but I have never bothered. Healthy plants are usually either unaffected or shrug the problem off. If confronted by a severely disfigured plant, I would be more likely to replace it with something tougher, and completely different.

Another category of blemishes is caused by pests, which take chunks from leaves and petals but are often long gone by the time their mysterious holes are discovered. The best detective work is carried out under cover of dark, when a torch will often reveal a culprit in the shape of a slug, caterpillar or earwig feeding nocturnally, in

the living garden

which case they can be quickly despatched by hand or foot. Around plants like dahlias, it is worth filling a small plastic flowerpot with loosely scrunched newspaper and balancing it, upside down, on a plant cane among the plants. During daytime, earwigs will rest in the newspaper and can be pulled out and squashed.

Sooty mould and scale insect

A black, sooty coating on leaf surfaces is sure to raise concern, but it is not, in itself, the prime offender. Sooty mould feeds on a sticky honeydew secreted by sap-sucking insects. These true culprits can usually be found on the undersides of leaves and the worst offenders are aphids or scale insects. Camellias, bay trees and citrus are particularly susceptible to scale. If you find the stems and veins colonized by small greenish brown scales, spray the pests with the relevant pesticide. Horticultural soft soap is an effective alternative to stronger chemicals, but whatever you use will require several applications to work. In time, new growth will replace that covered by the mould.

Aphids

Many folk work themselves into a lather over aphids (greenfly or blackfly), but the gardener with little time to spare needs to be made of sterner stuff. Aphids may cause yellowing, distortion, leaf curl and sooty mould, and spread viruses from one plant to another, but I still refuse to loose sleep over them. I usually squash newly spotted infestations by hand and sometimes ignore them, allowing my feathered friends to clean them up for me. Birds like blue tits, wrens and hedge sparrows eat aphids. Parasitization by wasps leaves a brown aphid husk behind. Hoverfly larvae, and lacewings and ladybirds and their larvae, all mop up aphids. Interestingly, if left, aphid colonies often disappear quite quickly. This is probably the result not just of predation and parasitism, but also because the colony seems to burn itself out. If you can't wait around for this to happen, the specific aphicide Pirimicarb is an effective pesticide to use.

Vine weevil

One of the most feared garden pests is vine weevil, which is particularly troublesome with potted or

Aphids are often highlighted by the antics of ants, running up and down the stems. These 'milk' the aphids of honeydew and even move them from place to place.

containerized plants. Vine weevils love fuchsias, cyclamen and primulas. The pity is that treasured plants usually collapse and die before the gardener realizes there is a problem. A post mortem will reveal a clutch of pale, 'C'-shaped larvae with brown heads around the roots. The adults, all female, are small, dark beetles about 9mm/⅓in long with elbow-shaped antennae. These come out at night to nibble notches from the edges of leaves. Stamping on the adult beetles is an effective way of reducing the numbers of eggs laid.

One or two incidences of vine weevil damage in a garden is nothing to worry about (in my last garden, numbers remained insignificent for ten years). However, if incidences increase, take action. Pesticides containing Imidacloprid provide an effective control. This is available in a potting compost or can be applied as a drench. For those like me avoiding pesticides, there is biological control in the shape of millions of tiny nematodes (microscopic soil organisms), which are watered into the compost during late summer and kill the larvae.

Slugs and snails

The unfortunate truth is that whatever we do, we can never get rid of all the slugs and snails in our gardens and neither should we want to, as they are part of the garden's ecology. Therefore the only logical action is to do our best to protect vulnerable plants – hosta, delphinium, French marigolds and runner bean seedlings being prime examples.

Slugs and snails dislike crossing rough, dry substances, so the first line of defence is barriers of coarse bark, sharp grit, soot and ash, arranged around plants.

There are proprietary slug killers on the market, of which the best known are probably slug pellets containing methiocarb or metaldehyde.

Hostas are a favourite food of slugs, who destroy the beauty of their foliage. But they do not find tough-leaved varieties such as 'Halcyon' or 'Sum and Substance' so palatable.

These are toxic and as such, I have not used them for years, because our garden is also used by cats, our dog, small children, birds and possibly hedgehogs and badgers. If you must put them down, use sparingly, one every 15cm/6in around vulnerable plants. Other slug killers based on aluminium sulphate are safer to use where pets and children are about. Personally, I avoid planting susceptible plants and use decoys and traps to protect others. Slugs and snails usually hole up somewhere safe and secure during daytime and ooze out at night to feed. Go out with a torch and you see armies of them sliming towards your runner beans, usually from one direction. Pick them up and destroy them, or place the traps and decoys between their hideaways and the plants. Containers half-filled with beer and sunk in the ground make good traps (both attracting and drowning the slugs), as do orange and grapefruit peel, with a little fruit still attached. A few decoy lettuce leaves may stop some in their tracks.

There is a biological control based on nematodes. Applied to the soil during spring and autumn, these enter the slugs' bodies and release bacteria which infect the slugs. This protection lasts for about six weeks and is useful if, say, you want to protect a vulnerable crop or seedbed. Unfortunately, it is not as effective against snails, because they have less contact with soil.

Rose problems

Most rose varieties are susceptible to black spot, mildew and rust, which return to infect them year after year, though not always all three at a time. The gardener short of time has three choices. Either put up with the rose diseases but enjoy the flowers anyway. Healthy roses are unlikely to die and generally manage to bloom, and although they may lose leaves in midsummer, these will regrow. It is possible to keep roses clean or almost clean by spraying with the relevant fungicides, which are available in cocktail form. It is important to begin spraying as soon as the foliage unfurls in spring, repeating two weeks later and two weeks later again. The alternative to these solutions is to grow only roses that are disease tolerant or resistant. Examples include repeat-flowering, fragrant shrub rose 'Roseraie de l'Haÿ' and the pink-flowered ground-cover rose 'Flower Carpet'.

Apple and pear tree problems

First, I would like to praise apple and pear trees in the garden. They make lovely features and act as a mecca for wildlife. The fact that they have pests and diseases makes them attractive to a wide range of birds including blue tits, long-tailed tits and woodpeckers, which eat pests and their eggs and beetle grubs from decaying bark. Blemished and fallen fruit provide autumn and winter fodder for late butterflies, pheasants, blackbirds, fieldfares and redwings. Although we are persuaded to prune out dead wood and clear up windfalls and rotten fruit, and many like to clean their trees up with a winter wash, I will have none of that and prefer to share my trees with garden wildlife.

Nevertheless, gardeners do worry over blemished leaves and fruits, most of which are caused by apple scab and closely related pear scab. It is possible to control this disease by spraying with fungicides. But for me, the chief joy of owning apple trees is being able to pick and eat fruit which I know has not been sprayed with anything. Unsprayed, our three varieties of eaters still supply us with fruit from August until February (with storing). Personally, I am happy to put up with a few scabby bits here and there – we simply cut them off and eat the rest of the apple. Collecting up and disposing of leaves cuts down on infection, as does thinning out congested branches to allow air and light into the tree, a task undertaken during winter (see pages 38–9). We had one tree with horribly scabby fruit, which we grubbed out. It will be replaced by a variety showing scab resistance like 'Red Devil' or 'Laxton's Superb'. A strong pear variety is 'Jargonelle'.

Canker is noticeable on bark, where patches sink inwards, causing flaking and decaying. This disease mostly affects older trees in poor health, especially those growing on badly drained soils. Common sense will tell you to cut out the worst affected parts and dispose of them away from the garden.

The following are just a few of many other smaller problems affecting fruit trees. Should young pears drop prematurely, suspect pear midge. Fallen fruitlets will contain tiny maggots and must be gathered up and disposed of quickly before the maggots go into the soil to pupate. Breaking the cycle will reduce next year's infestation.

Codling moth caterpillars tunnel into apple and pear fruits during summer, leaving them rotten in the middle by the time they are ripe. At this point the caterpillars exit the fruit to overwinter under the bark. Pheromone traps hung in the trees during spring trap male moths and prevent them from fertilizing females, thus reducing the eggs laid. Some gardeners tie strips of corrugated card around the tree trunks to see how many caterpillars they can collect during late summer, thus breaking the cycle.

Winter moths give rise to looper caterpillars which eat the leaves of fruit trees. They have an interesting life cycle involving female moths which cannot fly. Grease bands fitted to tree trunks in mid-autumn trap the female moths as they crawl up to prevent them from laying eggs.

Ladybirds are useful allies, as they and their lizard-like larvae eat countless aphids.

Nutrient deficiencies

Considering the range of plants we grow in our gardens, from all over the world, they give us remarkably few nutrient-related problems. When plants are in trouble, they are usually good at letting us know.

Magnesium deficiency, for instance, is commonly shown by obvious yellowing between the veins. A dose of Epsom salts applied as a foliar spray or to the roots should work miracles. Once when, more mysteriously, a *Prunus serrula* suddenly started dropping leaves in early summer, we suspected magnesium deficiency, applied Epsom salts and the problem stopped abruptly.

Iron (and to an extent, manganese) deficiency is another common problem, starting as a general yellowing of the leaves, which then turn brown at the edges, more markedly on young growth. This is a particular problem on acid-loving plants growing in alkaline soils. Rhododendrons and skimmias frequently show symptoms. Apart from choosing the right plants for the soil, you can ameliorate the condition by applying chelated iron. A liquid feed especially formulated for acid-loving plants usually contains both these elements in the correct form and others too.

Index

Figures in *italics* refer to captions

A

abelia 166
Abutilon vitifolium 150
  A. × *suntense* 150
  A. × *s.* 'Gorer's White' 150
  A. × *s.* 'Ralph Gould' 150
Acanthus mollis (bear's breeches) *77*,
  105, *105*, 134
  A. spinosus 134
Acer conspicuum 'Phoenix' 154
  A. grosseri var. *hersii* (Chinese snake
    bark) 30, 154
  A. palmatum 32
  A. pensylvanicum 'Erythrocladum'
    (moosewood) 14, 154, *154*
Adiantum pedatum 90
Agapanthus 139
agastache 24
Ajuga reptans (bugle) 68, 87
  A.r. 'Atropurpurea' *96*
Alchemilla mollis (lady's mantle) 15,
  134, *134*
  A. fulgens 134
Alisma plantago-aquatica (water
  plantain) 92, *92*, 93
Allium 12, 15, 26, 68
  A. cristophii (ornamental onion) 118,
    124, *124*
  A. hollandicum 'Purple Sensation'
    124
  A. schoenoprasum (chives) 130
  A. sphaerocephalon 124
  A. tuberosum (garlic chives) 130
Alocasia (giant taro) 105, *105*
Amaryllis belladonna 126
Amelanchier 14
  A. laevus 154
  A. lamarckii 154, *154*
  A. × *grandiflora* 'Ballerina' 154
Anaphalis margaritacea (pearl
  everlasting) 34, *35*
Anchusa azurea 'Loddon Royalist' 68
Anemone hupehensis 'Splendens' 134,
  134
  A. × *hybrida* 'Elegans' 134
  A. × *h.* 'Honorine Jobert' 134
annuals 15, 100, 127–9
  sowing 15, 25, 71
Anthemis (chamomile)
  A. tinctoria 'E. C. Buxton' 135
    A.t. 'Sauce Hollandaise' 134–5

A.t. 'Wargrave Variety' 135
aphids 158, 159, *159*, 167, *167*
apple trees 13, *39*, 155, *158*
  planting 30–1
  problems 169–70
  pruning 38–9
aquatic plants *see* ponds
Aquilegia (columbine) 71, 89
  A. alpina 135
  A. McKana Group 135
  A. vulgaris 89
    A.v. 'Firewheel' 135, *135*
archangel *see Lamium*
Argyranthemum (marguerite) 15, 108
  A. 'Cornish Gold' 127
  A. 'Jamaica Primrose' 127
  A. 'Summer Stars' 127
Artemisia 'Powis Castle' 47
Arum italicum 'Marmoratum' (lords and
  ladies) 135, *135*
arum lily *see Zantedeschia*
Asplenium scolopendrium (hart's tongue
  fern) 90, 132
  A.s. 'Crispum Bolton's Nobile' 132
Aster novi-belgii (Michaelmas daisy) 34
astilbe 9
Astrantia major 'Hadspen Blood' 52–3,
  135
  A.m. subsp. *involucrata* 'Shaggy' 135
  A.m. 'Sunningdale Variegated' 135
Athyrium 90

B

bamboo: screening 84, *84*, 94
  see Bashania, Chusquea, Phyllostachys
banana plants *see Musa basjoo*
bark
  composted 23
  mulch 66
Bashania fargesii (bamboo) 98
baskets, willow-weave herb 114, *114*
bay trees 64, 167
bear's breeches *see Acanthus*
beech *see Fagus sylvatica*
Berberis thunbergii f. *atropurpurea 40*
  B. × *stenophylla* 62
bergamot *see Monarda didyma*
Bergenia (elephant's ears) 15, 68, 164
  B. 'Bressingham White' 136
  B. 'Morgenrite' 136
  B. 'Silberlicht' 136

B. 'Sunningdale' 136
Betula (birch) 14, 30
  B. ermanii (Erman's birch) 154
  B. pendula (silver birch) 154
    B.p. 'Youngii' 154
  B. utilis var. *jaquemontii* 154
biennials *14*, 14–15, 24, 127–9
bindweed 164
birch *see Betula*
birds 10, 38, 39, 77, 158, 159, 167, 169
black-eyed Susan *see Rudbeckia*
blackfly *see* aphids
bluebell *see Hyacinthoides*
borders 9, 17, *17*, *18*
  digging 19, 22, 23, *23*
  maintenance 48, 52–3, 68, 72
Boston ivy *see Parthenocissus*
Bowles' golden grass *see Milium effusum*
  'Aureum'
box *see Buxus*
  box balls 64–5, *65*
Brachyglottis 'Drysdale (Senecio) 142
  B. 'Sunshine' 142
broom *see Cytisus*
buckthorn *see Rhamnus*
Buddleja davidii (butterfly bush) 10
  B.d. 'Black Knight' 142
  B.d. 'Dartmoor' 142
  B.d. 'White Profusion' 142
bugle *see Ajuga reptans*
bulbs 15, 52, 26–7, 124–6, 166
butterflies, flowers for 10, *35*, 142, 169
butterfly bush *see Buddleja*
Buxus sempervirens (box) 32, 62, 64–5,
  65, 110, 142, *142*
  B. s. 'Marginata' 142

C

Calamintha nepeta 'White Cloud' (lesser
  catmint) 94
Calendula officinalis 100
camellias 22, 61, 161, 167
Campanula 15
  C. lactiflora 'Loddon Anna' 56–7, *57*
canker 169–70
Canna 72, 117, *117*
  C. 'Black Knight' 127
  C. 'Panache' 127
  C. 'Wyoming' 127
Cape figwort *see Phygelius capensis*
Carex 98

Caryopteris 14
    C. × *clandonensis* 'Heavenly Blue' 142
    C. × *c.* 'Worcester Gold' 142
caterpillars 166, 170
catmint *see Calamintha nepeta, Nepeta*
Cerastium tomentosum (snow-in-
    summer) *110*
Ceratophyllum demersum (hornwort) 92
Chaenomeles (japonica, Japanese quince)
    34, 40, *58*, 58–9
    C. × *speciosa* 'Moerloosei' 150
Chamaecyparis lawsoniana 'Summer
    Snow' 118
chamomile *see Anthemis*
cherry *see Prunus*
Chilean glory flower *see Eccremocarpus
    scaber*
Chilean potato vine *see Solanum*
Chinese snake bark *see Acer*
chives *see Allium*
Choisya: C. 'Aztec Pearl' 143
    C. ternata (Mexican orange) 142–3
Christmas rose *see Helleborus niger*
Chusan palm *see Trachycarpus fortunei*
Chusquea culeou 132
    C.c. 'Tenuis' 132
Cirsium rivulare 'Atropurpureum' 138
clarkia 15
Clematis 16, 40, *40*, 42–3
    C. armandii 42, 43
    C. 'Etoile Violette' 150
    C. 'Helsingbord' 150, *150*
    C. 'Jackmanii Rubra' 106
    C. macropetala 150
    C. montana 42
    C. 'Nelly Moser' 40
    C. 'Niobe' *106*
    C. viticella 150
    C. × *durandii* 15, 144
climbing plants 15–16, 84, 150–3
    pruning 40
    training 41
cloches, bottle *102*
columbine *see Aquilegia*
compost 22, 23, 161, 162–3, *165*
coneflower *see Echinacea, Rudbeckia*
container plants 32–3, 61, 86, 108–9
corkscrew hazel *see Corylus avellana*
corms *see bulbs*
cornflowers 15
Cornus (dogwood) 15, *72*
    C. alba 'Sibirica' 143, *143*
    C. alba 'Spaethii' 143
    C. sanguinea 'Midwinter Fire' 143
    C. stolonifera 'Flaviramea' 143
Corylus avellana 'Contorta' (corkscrew
    hazel) 143
Cosmos sulphureus 100

Cotinus coggygria 144
    C.c. 'Grace' 144
    C.c. 'Royal Purple' 143–4
Cotoneaster 72
    C. divaricatus 144
    C. horizontalis 151
    C. simonsii 74, 75, 144
cotton lavender *see Santolina chamaecy
    parissus*
couch grass 164
courgettes 102, *102*, 130
courtyard gardens 10, 13, 94–5
    see also container plants
crab apple *see Malus*
cranesbill *see Geranium*
Crataegus (hawthorn, may) 10
    C. laevigata 'Paul's Scarlet' 154–5
    C.l. 'Plena' 155
    C. pedicellata 155
    C. × *lavalleei* 'Carrierei' 155
Crocosmia 'Lucifer' (montbretia) 117
Crocus 26–7, 80
    C. chrysanthus 'Prins Claus' 124
    C.c. 'Prinses Beatrix' 124
    C.c. 'Snow Bunting' 124, *124*
    C.c. 'Zwanenburg Bronze' 124
Cupressocyparis leylandii (Leyland
    cypress) 62, 64
Cupressus macrocarpa 'Green Pillar' 118
    C. sempervirens 64
    C.s. 'Swane's Gold' 155
    C.s. 'Totem Pole' 155
currant, flowering *see Ribes*
cypress *see Cupressus, Cupressocyparis*
Cytisus 161
    C. battandieri 150

D
daffodils *see Narcissus*
Dahlia 72, 167
    D. 'Bishop of Llandaff' 117, *117*,
    127, *127*
    D. 'Chimborazo' 127
    D. 'David Howard' 127
daisies *see Argyranthemum, Aster novi-
    belgii*
Darley Dale heath *see Erica*
Darmera peltata 105
deadheading 15, 68, *73*
Deutzia 68
Dianthus (pinks) 68, *110*
Dicentra 'Stuart Boothman' 52
digging 19, 22, 23, *23*
Digitalis (foxglove) 14, *14*, 24, 47, 71
    D. Excelsior Group 127
    D. parviflora 127
    D. purpurea 127
    D.p. f. *albiflora* 127

diseases 19, 159
division, propagation by 34, 54
dogwood *see Cornus*
Doronicum (leopard's bane) 80
Dryopteris felix-mas (male fern) 90

E
earwigs 166, 167
Eccremocarpus scaber (Chilean glory
    flower) *9*
Echinacea purpurea (purple coneflower)
    136, *136*
    E.p. 'Magnus' 136
    E.p. 'White Lustre' 136
Echinops (globe thistle)
    E. bannaticus 'Taplow Blue' 136
    E. ritro 'Veitch's Blue' 136
Elaeagnus pungens 'Maculata' 144
    E. 'Quicksilver' 144, 155
    E. × *ebbingei* 18, 144
    E. × *e.* 'Gilt Edge' 113, *113*, 144
elephant's ears *see Bergenia*
Epimedium perralderianum 143
Eremurus stenophyllus (foxtail lily) 118
Erica carnea 'Springwood White' 144
    E. × *darleyensis* 'White Perfection'
    (Darley Dale heath, winter-
    flowering heather) 144
Eryngium (sea holly)
    E. alpinum 136
    E. bourgatii 118
    E. giganteum 136
    E. × *oliverianum* 136
Euonymus alatus 144, *144*
    E. europaeus 'Red Cascade' 144–5
    E. fortunei 34
    E.f. 'Emerald Gaiety' 145
    E.f. 'Emerald 'n' Gold' 15, 82, 145,
    145
    E.f. 'Silver Queen' 150–1
Eupatorium purpureum (Joe Pye weed)
    117
Euphorbia 68,
E. amygdaloides var. *robbiae* (Mrs Robb's
    bonnet) 82, 137
    E. characias 137
    E.c. subsp. *wulfenii* 136–7
    E. dulcis 'Chameleon' 87
    E. polychroma 80, 137
    E. × *martinii* 137
eye-lashed fern *see Polytichum polyble
    pharum*

F
Fagus sylvatica (beech) 62, 64
Fatsia japonica 113, *117*
feather grass *see Stipa tenuissima*
fences 84

fennel *see Foeniculum vulgare*
ferns 14, 15, 90, 132–3
    tree *13*
fertilizers 60–1, 160, 166
Festuca gautieri 132
    F. glauca 'Blaufuchs' (blue fescue) 98, 132
    F.g. 'Elijah Blue' 132
    F.g. 'Golden Toupee' 132
feverfew *see Tanacetum parthenium*
firethorn *see Pyracantha*
foam flower (*Tiarella wherryi*) 82
Foeniculum vulgare (fennel) 114, 118, *118*
foliage plants 105
foliar feeds, applying 60
fountain grass *see Pennisetum*
foxglove *see Digitalis*
foxtail lily *see Eremurus stenophyllus*
French beans 24, 25, 102, 130
Fritillaria meleagris (snakeshead fritillary) 27
fruit trees *see* apple trees, pear trees
Fuchsia 168
    F. 'Alice Hoffman' 145
    F. magellanica 145
      F.m. var. *gracilis* 'Tricolor' *57*
    F. 'Riccartonii' 145

G

Galanthus (snowdrop)
    G. 'Magnet' 124
    G. nivalis 26, 120, *120*, 124
      G.n. 'Flore Pleno' 124
    G. 'S. Arnott' 124
Galium odoratum (woodruff) *90*
garlic chives *see Allium tuberosum*
Gazania 'Kiss' 128
    G. 'Talent' 128
Geranium (cranesbill) 15, 68, 76
    G. endressii 52
    G. 'Johnson's Blue' 68
    G. magnificum 47, 68
    G. palmatum 164
    G. psilostemon (Armenian cranesbill) 137, *137*
    G. sanguineum 137
gladioli 26
globe thistle *see Echinops*
grasses *4*, 14, 15, *66*, 132–3
greenfly *see* aphids
ground cover plants 15, 18, 96–7
ground elder 164, *165*

H

hairy canary clover *see Lotus hirsutus*
Hamamelis (witch hazel)
    H. × *intermedia* 'Diane' 145
    H. × *i.* 'Jelena' 145

H. × *i.* 'Pallida' 145, *145*
Harry Lauder's walking stick *see Corylus avellana*
hart's tongue fern *see Asplenium scolopendrium*
hawthorn *see Crataegus*
heathers 15, 18
    see Erica
Hebe 'Great Orme' 146
    H. 'Midsummer Beauty' 146
    H. pinguifolia 'Pagei' 120, *120*
Hedera (ivy)
    H. colchica 'Sulphur Heart' 151
    H. helix 120, *120*
      H.h. 'Atropurpurea' 151
      H.h. 'Buttercup' 151
      H.h. 'Luzii' 151
hedges 9, 10, 62–3
    topiary 64
Helianthemum (sun rose)
    H. 'Rhodanthe Carneum' 146
    H. 'Wisley Primrose' 146
    H. 'Wisley White' 146
Helichrysum 108
Helleborus (hellebore)
    H. argutifolius (Corsican hellebore) 14, 137, *137*
    H. foetidus (stinking hellebore) 137
    H. hybridus 137
    H. niger (Christmas rose) 137
herbs 130–1
    in baskets 114, *114*
Hesperis matronalis (sweet rocket) 14, 24, 89, *89*
holly, hedgehog *see Ilex aquifolium*
honesty *see Lunaria annua*
honeysuckle *see Lonicera*
    Himalayan *see Leycesteria formosa*
hop, golden 94
Hordeum jubatum 4
hornwort *see Ceratophyllum demersum*
horsetail, field 165
Hosta 98, *98*, 168, *168*
Hyacinthoides hispanica (Spanish bluebell) 82
    H. non-scripta (common bluebell) 82
Hydrangea 94
    H. anomala subsp. *petiolaris* 151
    H. arborescens 'Annabelle' 146
    H. macrophylla 'Lanarth White' 146, *146*
hyssop *110*

I

ice plant *see Sedum*
Ilex aquifolium 'Ferox Argentea' 147
    I.a. 'Ferox Aurea' (hedgehog holly) 146, *146*

Ipomoea tricolor 'Heavenly Blue' 84, *84*
Iris 89, *89*
    I. 'Alcazar' (bearded iris) 138, *138*
    I. 'Cantab' 124–5, *125*
    I. danfordiae 120, *120*
    I. ensata 92
    I. laevigata 'Variegata' 98
    I. latifolia (English iris) 125
    I. pallida 'Variegata' 87, 138
    I. sibirica (Siberian iris) 138
iron deficiency 160, 170
Itea ilicifolia 113
ivy *see Hedera*
    Boston ivy *see Parthenocissus*

J

Japanese anemone 164
Japanese knotweed *see Persicaria japonica*
Japanese quince *see Chaenomeles*
japonica *see Chaenomeles*
Jasminum (jasmine)
    J. nudiflorum (winter jasmine) 40, 76, 151
    J. officinale 40, 151
Joe Pye weed *see Eupatorium*
Juncus effusus (soft rush) 87
juneberry *see Amelanchier*

K

Knautia macedonica (scabious) 15, 138, *138*
Kniphofia (red hot poker) *139*
    K. caulescens 138
    K. 'Percy's Pride' 138
    K. rooperi 138

L

laburnum, evergreen *see Piptanthus*
ladybirds 158, 167, *170*
lady's mantle *see Alchemilla*
Lagarosiphon major (pondweed) 55, *55*, 92
Lamium galeobdolon (archangel) 82
    L. orvala 82
Lantana camara 108
Lathyrus odoratus (sweet pea) 16, 25, 128
    L.o. 'Wiltshire Ripple' 128, *128*
laurel hedges 62
laurustinus *see Viburnum tinus*
Lavandula (lavender) 15, 62, *67*, 68, *102*, 110, *110*, 161
    L. angustifolia 'Loddon Anna' 147
      L.a. 'Loddon Blue' 147, *147*
      L.a. 'Munstead' 110
    L. stoechas (French lavender) 110, 118, 147
    L. × *intermedia* (English lavender) 110

lawns 10, *10*, 12, *12*
  converting to bed 23
  edges 51, 77
  maintenance 50, 77
layering shrubs 34, 82
leaf mould 22
leaves
  blemished 166–7
  fallen 77
lemon thyme *see Thymus × citriodorus*
leopard's bane *see Doronicum*
lettuce, red-leaved 102
Leucanthemum × superbum (shasta daisy) 34
Leucojum aestivum (summer snowflake) 80
Leycesteria formosa (Himalayan honeysuckle) 147
Leyland cypress *see Cupressocyparis leylandii*
lilies *see Eremurus, Lilium, Zantedeschia*
Lilium (lily) 26, 68
  L. 'Casa Blanca' 94–5, *95*, 125
  L. longiflorum 94–5
  L. 'Marco Polo' 94, 125
  L. regale 94, 125
Linaria vulgaris (toadflax) 66
lobelia 108
Lonicera (honeysuckle) 16, 34, 40, 76
  L. caprifolium 152
  L. nitida 68
    L.n. 'Baggesen's Gold' *68*
  L. periclymenum 'Belgica' (Dutch honeysuckle) 40, 152
    L.p. 'Graham Thomas' 152
    L.p. 'Serotina' *151*, 151–2
  L. × americana 152
lords and ladies *see Arum italicum*
Lotus hirsutus (hairy canary clover) *67*, 147
love-in-a-mist *see Nigella damascena*
Luma apiculata 'Glanleam Gold' (myrtle) 28
Lunaria annua (honesty) 14, *16*, 24, 48–9, *49*, 118, 128
  L.a. var. *albiflora* 128
  L.a. 'Variegata' 128
lungwort *see Pulmonaria*
lupin 24, 159
Lychnis coronaria (rose campion) *17*, 48–9, 71,138–9
  L. flos-jovis 139
  L. viscaria (German catchfly) 139

M
magnesium deficiency 160, 170
Magnolia stellata 147, 166
  M.s. 'Waterlily' 147

M. × loebneri 'Merrill' 147
Mahonia aquifolium (Oregon grape) 147
  M. × m. 'Buckland' 147
  M. × media 'Charity' 76, 147
Malus 'Golden Hornet' (crab apple) 26
manure 22–3, 161
maple *see Acer*
Marguerite *see Argyranthemum*
marjoram *see Origanum vulgare*
marrows 130
Matteuccia struthiopteris (shuttlecock fern) 132, *132*
may *see Crataegus*
Melianthus major 117
Mexican orange *see Choisya ternata*
Michaelmas daisy *see Aster novi-belgii*
Milium effusum 'Aureum' (Bowles' golden grass) 98
mock orange *see Philadelphus*
Monarda didyma (bergamot) 24, 34
montbretia *see Crocosmia*
moosewood *see Acer pensylvanicum*
mould, sooty 167
mountain ash *see Sorbus*
mulching *22*, 60, 66–7
mullein *see Verbascum*
Musa basjoo (banana) 13, 105, *105*
mushroom compost 23
myrtle *see Luma apiculata*

N
Narcissus (daffodil) 26, 27, *27*, *49*, 52, 80, 166
  N. 'Ice Follies' 126
  N. 'Jack Snipe' 126
  N. 'Jetfire' 125, *125*
  N. 'Tête-à-tête' 120, *120*, 125–6
nasturtiums 24
Nectaroscordum siculum 118
Nepeta (catmint): *N.* 'Six Hills Giant' 139
  N. × faassenii 139
Nerine bowdenii 26, 126, *126*
New Zealand flax *see Phormium*
Nicotiana alata (tobacco plant) 95, 128
  N. langsdorffii 128
  N. sylvestris 128
Nigella damascena (love-in-a-mist) 15, 24, 25, *25*, 129
  N.d. 'Miss Jekyll' *128*, 129
nutrient deficiencies 160, 170
Nymphaea 'Pygmaea Helvola' (pygmy water lily) 98

O
obelisks 106
onions, ornamental *see Allium*
Oregon grape *see Mahonia aquifolium*
Origanum vulgare (marjoram) 114

Osmanthus delavayi 148
  O. heterophyllus 'Aureomarginatus' 147
  O. × burkwoodii 148
oxygenating plants 55, 92, 93

P
Papaver (poppy) 15
  P. orientale (oriental poppy) 'Beauty of Livermere' 139
  P.o. 'Cedric Morris' 139
  P.o. 'Mrs Perry' 139, *139*
  P. somniferum (opium poppy) *70*
Parthenocissus quinquefolia (Virginia creeper) 40, 152
  P. tricuspidata (Boston ivy) 152
Passiflora (passion flower) 40
  P. caerulea 152
    P.c. 'Constance Elliot' 152
  P. incarnata (Maypops) 152
  P. 'Incense' 152
pear trees 13
  planting 30–1
  problems 169–70
  pruning 38–9
  see also Pyrus
pearl everlasting *see Anaphalis margaritacea*
Pennisetum alopecuroides 'Hameln' 133, *133*
  P. orientale 133
Penstemon 68
  P. 'Andenken an Friedrich Hahn' 140
  P. 'Appleblossom' 140
  P. 'Evelyn' 139–40
  P. heterophyllus 140
perennials 14, 15, 118, 127–9
  dividing 34, *35*
  sowing 71
  transplanting 52–3
Persicaria japonica (Japanese knotweed) 164
pests and pesticides 19, 39, 159, 166–9
  see also slugs, snails
Petunia Grandiflora Group 94, *95*
  P. 'Million bells' 108
  P. 'Ultra Rose Star' 129
Philadelphus (mock orange) 68, 166
  P. 'Beauclerk' 148, *148*
  P. 'Belle Etoile' 148
  P. 'Manteau d'Hermine' 148
Phlomis cashmeriana 140
  P. fruticosa 140
  P. russeliana 140
Phlox paniculata 'Eva Cullum' 140
  P.p. 'Fujiyama' 140
  P.p. 'Graf Zeppelin' 140
Phormium (New Zealand flax)
  P. cookianum 33

P. 'Maori Sunrise' 148
P. 'Sundowner' 149
P. tenax 32, *67*, *117*, 148
Phygelius capensis (Cape fig-wort) 32, 148
P. 'Sensation' 148
P. × *rectus* 'Moonraker' 148
Phyllostachys (bamboo) 113, *113*
    P. aureosulcata 'Spectabilis' (yellow-groove bamboo) 133
    P. nigra 133
pine cone mulch 66, *66*
Pines flexilis 'Firmament' (dwarf limber pine) 148
    P. mugo (dwarf mountain pine) 32, 148
    P.m. 'Mops' 148
    P. sylvestris 'Beuvronensis' (dwarf Scots pine) 148
pinks see *Dianthus*
Piptanthus nepalensis (laburnum) 150
Pittosporum 86, 94, *113*, 161
    P. tenuifolium 153
plants, choosing 13–16
Platycodon grandiflorus 118
Polygonatum (Solomon's seal) 80, *80*
Polystichum polyblepharum (eye-lashed fern) 133
    P. setiferum (soft shield fern) 133
ponds 54–5, 92–3
pondweed see *Lagarosiphon major*
pool, miniature 98, *98*
poppies see *Papaver*
porches 120, *120*
potting on 32–3
propagation 34, 54, 82
    see also seed
pruning
    fruit trees 38–9
    roses 7, 40, 46–7, 73
    shrubs 19, 68, 74–5, 166
Prunus incisa 'Kojo-no-mai' (Fuji cherry) 32
Pulmonaria (lungwort) 15
    P. 'Mawson's Blue' 140
    P. rubra 'Redstart' 140
    P. saccharata 'Leopard' *90*, 140
    P.s. 'Mrs Moon' 140
    P. 'Sissinghurst White' 140
pumpkin 130
Pyracantha 'Teton' (firethorn) *152*, 152–3
Pyrus communis 'Doyenné du Comice' (pear) 155, *155*
    P. salicifolia 'Pendula' (weeping silver pear) 155

R
raised beds 67
red hot poker see *Kniphofia*

Rhamnus alaternus 'Argenteovariegata' (variegated Italian buckthorn) 153
Rhododendron 22, 61, 160, 161, 170
    R. yakushimanum 32
Ribes (flowering currant)
    R. alpinum 'Aureum' 149
    R. sanguineum 'Brocklebankii' 149
rice-paper plant see *Tetrapanax papyrifer*
rock gardens 10
rocket
    salad 131
    sweet see *Hesperis matronalis*
Rosa (rose) 7, 16, 40, 46–7, 73, *159*, 169
    R. 'Alchymist' 153
    R. 'Climbing Etoile de Hollande' 153, *153*
    R. 'Felicia' 149
    R. 'Flower Carpet' 169
    R. glauca 118
    R. 'Madame Alfred Carrière' 153
    R. 'New Dawn' 153
    R. 'Penelope' 149
    R. 'Pink Bells' *106*
    R. 'Roseraie de l'Hay' 169
    R. rugosa hedges 62
rose campion see *Lychnis coronaria*
rosemary see *Rosmarinus*
roses see *Rosa*
Rosmarinus officinalis (rosemary) 62
    R.o. 'Miss Jessopp's Upright' 130
    R.o. 'Primley Blue' 130
    R.o. 'Roseus' 130
rowan see *Sorbus*
Rudbeckia (coneflower) 15, 68
    R. fulgida var. *sullivantii* 'Goldsturm' *4*, *140*, 141
    R.f. var. *deamii* 141
    R. hirta 'Goldilocks' 129
    R.h. 'Marmalade' 100, 129
    R.h. 'Rustic Dwarfs' 129, *129*
runner beans 158
    'Hestia' 130, *130*
    'Pickwick' 130
rush see *Juncus*

S
Salvia (sage)
    S. forsskaolii 17, 71
    S. officinalis 86–7, 131
    S.o. 'Icterina' 87, 131
    S.o. Purpurascens 114, 131
    S.o. 'Tricolor' 114, 131
Salyx babylonica var. *pekinensis* 'Tortuosa' (twisted willow) 143
Santolina chamaecyparissus (cotton lavender) *110*
scabious see *Knautia macedonica*
scale insects 167

scented plants 94–5
Schizophragma integrifolium 151
Scilla (squill)
    S. mischtschenkoana 26, 126
    S. siberica (Siberian squill) 18, 126, *126*
screening, bamboo 84, *84*, 94
screens, evergreen 113
sea holly see *Eryngium*
seats 8, *8*
Sedum (ice plant)
    S. 'Herbstfreude' 141
    S. 'Ruby Glow' 96–7
    S. spectabile 34, *35*, *110*, 141
    S.s. 'Brilliant' 87, *141*
seed
    collecting 70–1
    sowing 15, *16*, 24–5, 71, *77*
seedlings, thinning 25, *25*, 48–9
Senecio see *Brachyglottis*
shasta daisy see *Leucanthemum* × *superbum*
shell mulch 66
shingle 13
    mulch 12, 66, *66*, 67, *67*
shrubs 13, 14
    planting 17–18, 28–9
    pruning 19, 68, 74–5, 166
    sowing seed 71
    transplanting 58–9
shuttlecock fern see *Matteuccia struthiopteris*
Sidalcea malviflora 'Elsie Heugh' *136*
silver birch see *Betula pendula*
skimmias 170
slugs 24, 102, *168*, 168–9
snails 24, 102, 168–9
snakeshead fritillary see *Fritillaria meleagris*
snow-in-summer see *Cerastium tomentosum*
snowdrop see *Galanthus*
snowy mespilus see *Amelanchier*
soft shield fern see *Polystichum setiferum*
soil 22, 160–1
    acid/alkaline 161
    conditioning 22–3, 68, 160
    digging 19, 22, 23, *23*
    nutrient deficiencies 160, 170
Solanum crispum (Chilean potato vine) 16, 40
    S.c. 'Glasnevin' 153
    S. laxum 16
    S.l. 'Album' 153
soldiers and sailors see *Pulmonaria*
Solomon's seal see *Polygonatum*
sooty mould 167

Sorbus aucuparia (rowan, mountain ash) 14, *71*, 155
    S. cashmiriana (Kashmir rowan) 155
    S. koehneana 155
    S. vilmorinii 155
spurge *see Euphorbia*
squash 130
staking
    plants *9*, 19, 56–7
    trees 30, 31
Stipa (feather grass)
    S. gigantea 133, *133*
    S. tenuissima 98, 133
suckers, transplanting 34, 58
summer snowflake *see Leucojum aestivum*
sun rose *see Helianthemum*
sunflowers 24
supports *see* staking
sweetcorn 102, *102*, 131
sweet pea *see Lathyrus odoratus*

T
Tagetes 100
Tanacetum parthenium (feverew) 114
taro, giant *see Alocasia*
Taxus baccata (yew) hedges 62–3, 64
Tetrapanax papyrifer (rice-paper plant) 105, *105*
Thymus vulgaris (thyme) 131
    T.v. 'Goldentiné' 131
    T.v. 'Silver Posie' 131
    T. × *citriodorus* (lemon thyme) 110, 131
Tiarella wherryi (foam flower) 82
toadflax, common *see Linaria vulgaris*
tobacco plant *see Nicotiana alata*
tomatoes 102
    'Sweet 100' 131, *131*

topiary 64–5, 68
Trachycarpus fortunei (Chusan palm) *117*
transplanting
    perennials 52–3
    shrubs 58–9
    trees 13–14, 82, 154–5
    planting 30–1
    staking 30, 31
    see also apple trees, pear trees
Tulipa (tulip) 15, 26, *26*, 52, 80–1
    T. 'Apricot Beauty' 126
    T. 'High Society' *80*, 126
    T. 'Johann Strauss' 126
    T. 'Queen of the Night' 126
    T. saxatalis 126
    T. 'Spring Green' 126
twisted nut *see Corylus avellana*

V
vegetables 9, 24, 102, 130–1
Verbascum (mullein) 14
    V. bombyciferum 129
    V. chaixii 57
        V.c. 'Gainsborough 129, *129*
    V. 'Snow Maiden' 129
Verbena bonariensis 141, *141*
    V. rigida 141
Veronicastrum virginicum f. *album* (white Culver's root) 117, *117*
Viburnum 72, 76
    V. farreri 34
    V. lantana (wayfaring tree) 62
    V. plicatum 96
    V. × *bodnantense* 'Charles Lamont' 149
        V. × *b.* 'Dawn' 149, *149*
        V. × *b.* 'Deben' 149
    Viburnum tinus 113, 149
        V.t. 'Eve Price' 149
        V.t. 'Lucidum' 149

Vinca difformis 68
vine weevils 167–8
Virginia creeper *see Parthenocissus*

W
wallflowers 14
water features 86
    see ponds, pool
water lilies 54, 55
    pygmy *see Nymphaea*
water plantain *see Alisma plantago-aquatica*
watering 60, 61
wayfaring tree *see Viburnum lantana*
weeds/weedkillers 12, 18, *18*, 19, 22, 23, 72, 164–5
    see also ground cover, mulching
'wigwams' *9*, 56, 106
wild planting 26–7, 82
willow, twisted *see Salyx*
winter-flowering plants 76
wisteria, pruning 44–5
Wisteria 40, 44–5, 166
    W. floribunda 153
    W. sinensis 153, *153*
        W.s. 'Alba' 153
witch hazel *see Hamamelis*
woodbine *see Lonicera*
woodruff *see Galium odoratum*
worms 158
wound paint 39

Y
yew *see Taxus baccata*

Z
Zantedeschia (arum lily) 105
Zinnia boliviensis 100

Publisher's Acknowledgments

Project editor Alison Freegard
Designer Ruth Prentice
Horticultural consultant Tony Lord
Indexer Vicky Robinson
Production Kim Oliver